Fantasy and Common Sense in Education

Fantasy and Common Sense in Education

JOHN WILSON

Department of Educational Studies
Oxford University

A HALSTED PRESS BOOK

John Wiley & Sons
New York

First published in 1979 by Martin Robertson & Co. Ltd., 108 Cowley Road, Oxford OX4 1JF.

Published in the U.S.A. by Halsted Press, a Division of John Wiley & Sons, New York

ISBN 0 470-26707-0

Library of Congress Cataloging in Publication Data

Wilson, John, 1928–
    Fantasy and common sense in education.

    "A Halsted Press book."
    Bibliography: p.
    1. Wilson, John, 1928–   2. Education—Philosophy.
    3. Fantasy. I. Title.
LB885.W5F36 1979   370.1   79–10938
ISBN 0–470–26707–0

Typeset by Pioneer Associates, East Sussex
Printed and bound in Britain by Richard Clay Ltd.
at The Chaucer Press, Bungay, Suffolk.

Contents

Preface

The genesis of this book may perhaps help the reader to understand, and (I hope) to view more favourably, its somewhat unusual nature. A more detailed account of the relationship between philosophy, fantasy and education is given in Part I: here I want simply to give a brief description of why the book has the form it does. (Some further remarks are contained in the Postscript.)

Anyone who is in the philosophy business for other than mere amusement must, I take it, want to improve (however indirectly) things in the practical world. Such a person may, of course, choose to tackle philosophical problems that are genuinely complex, and require a high degree of intellectual ability; and the domain marked by 'philosophy of education' certainly has some of these. However, he is bound to feel that many, perhaps most, of the things that go badly wrong in education are the result of (or correlate with) mistakes or false pictures that are, from the strictly intellectual viewpoint, extremely *simple*. As with the Nazis (to use an example that will reappear several times in this book), and many other cases where things go badly wrong, it is not that people are not *clever* enough: it is rather that they are not *reasonable* enough — a very different thing. In order for philosophy to be of much practical use, then, it must be mingled with some more general attempt to improve reasonableness: and this can only, or must chiefly, be done by trying to make people aware of the kinds of feelings, prejudices, false assumptions and (in particular) fantasies that inhibit rationality.

The difficulty of even trying to do this consists in getting the right admixture of strict philosophy — that is, very roughly, the formal or logical demonstration of distinctions and conceptual truths — on the one hand, and on the other hand some satisfactory description of the feelings and fantasies that people actually suffer from in relation to various topics. If one dispensed (as do nearly all philosophers, understandably) nothing but the former, only those already reasonable enough, and sufficiently acclimatised to philosophical thinking, would be likely to be at all influenced in their practical behaviour; on the other hand, if one cut out the logical proofs altogether and just described the fantasies, one would have offered no reason for believing that they were in fact *fantasies* rather than reasonably held ideas and beliefs.

No single book (perhaps no collection of books) can present the right admixture for everyone; indeed I doubt whether it would even make sense to demand this. It is, in practical living, a matter for nice and individual judgement to decide when, in Jane Austen's words, to pay someone 'the compliment of rational disagreement' and hence to *argue* with him on the assumption that he will be influenced by logic; and when, on the contrary, the person needs a kiss or a hug or a polite smile or a parable or a recommendation to a good psychoanalyst. Most of us — and of course I include professional philosophers in this group, which is why I hope that what I say will be of interest to them as well as to laymen — lie somewhere between the ideally rational Socrates, 'following the argument wheresoever it may lead', as Plato puts it, and the almost entirely irrational and non-negotiable Hitler or any other kind of lunatic. Different people, in other words, need different kinds of treatment at different times, and in respect of different topics or areas of life.

Nevertheless, I write partly at least because this *kind* of enterprise seems to me important (whether I conduct it well or badly), and hence it seems important both to sketch out in some detail what it in principle consists of and to offer at least some examples of it in practice. This book has that dual purpose. Accordingly, after having sketched the enterprise in general and said something about philosophy on the one hand and the major fantasies that beset us on the other, I shall take a heterogeneous set of examples and deal with them heterogeneously, in the hope that by casting my net sufficiently wide I shall offer everyone at least one or two cases of the right treatment. In other words, sometimes I shall want to argue in a fairly stringent philosophical way for a certain position, without considering in detail what fantasies tend to make us forget the force or conclusions of such arguments; at other times it may be profitable to confront the fantasies more directly, before proceeding very far with the philosophical analysis. For this multifarious procedure I make no apology, other than the foregoing.

Plato seems to have thought that the written word in some way corrupted or desensitised philosophy; and one certainly feels that, ideally, it would be better to discuss these topics on a person-to-person basis, under conditions of greater trust and less abstraction than exists between reader and author. The author sacrifices some of that closeness for the sake of a wider audience; and if this book does not justify such a sacrifice, I can plead only that it is (so far as I know) a first attempt in an extremely difficult interdisciplinary field. If it inspires other writers to do the job better, I shall be the first to applaud.

I owe a debt to many critics and advisers, too numerous to mention individually here; but I must acknowledge particular gratitude to Nancy Swift, for giving me some kind of grasp, however insecure, of the nature and powers of fantasy: and to my own students, for tolerating and monitoring my attempts to work with them in this field. Acknowledgements are also due to journals in which some of the material used in certain chapters originally appeared, though in most cases that material has been considerably revised: to the journal of the Philosophy Society for material in chapter 2, to *Educational Research* (edited and published by the National Foundation of Educational Research) for material in chapter 5, and to the *Oxford Review* for material in chapter 7 (see note on that chapter).

J.B.W.
Oxford, 1978

PART I

CHAPTER 1

A General Perspective

Education has been compared by some philosophers with love and other kinds of personal relationships (e.g. John Lucas in Bryan Wilson's collection, 1975, p. 39). That is certainly going too far: learning that is significantly above the level of nature, relevant to people as such, and intentionally promoted in a sustained and generalised sort of way — and these are, as I have shown elsewhere (J. Wilson, 1979), a sufficient set of conditions for the application of the term 'education' — can certainly go on without all the uncertainties, variations, unpredictability and lack of system that characterise intimate relationships between people. Nevertheless, some of this openness or uncertainty is inherent in many kinds of learning, including some of the most important, and is an inevitable background for almost all kinds. A very great deal of serious education is, to put it rather dramatically, much more like what happens between patient and therapist, admirer and hero, or child and parent than like what happens between trainee and trainer, or between the seeker for information and the informative computer or encyclopaedia. Essentially, education involves the interaction of one human mind or soul with another.

This tempts one to think, at least in some moods, that not much can be gained by *writing* about education at all. For how can one, in general terms and standing at such a distance from the reader, capture or transmit the significant features of what goes on — any more, as many therapists would claim, than one can describe in a textbook what goes on in a successful therapeutic session? Perhaps a good novelist might do it; but if the process is not, so to speak, generalisable or systematisable in any significant degree, what is there to say? One may remind the reader of truisms, or demolish the

1

pretensions of those educational theorists and others who try to make the business of education fit their particular entrenched expertises; but this hardly seems enough.

The trouble with this view is not that it is extremist: for the core or heart of education *is* like that, or sufficiently like it — whatever may be the case with such important but peripheral matters as the cost of school meals, the effects of comprehensive education on the British class system, and so forth. Rather the view omits *one* possible set of generalisations or general descriptions that *can* be made, though of a very different kind from those usually produced by educational theorists; just as, though personal relationships in general cannot be very helpfully discussed or systematised in terms of physiological stimuli, or of some restrictive and imperceptive morality, or of bureaucratic administration, or perhaps indeed of anything we should want to call a 'theory' at all, it would nevertheless be premature to conclude that nothing both general and useful can be said about them.

Nor is it hard to see in principle what kind of thing can be said. There will be certain characteristic virtues and vices, pieces of good sense and pieces of nonsense, reasonable and unreasonable approaches, perceptive and imperceptive ways of handling things in education, as in (other) personal relationships: the author's job will be to point these out. But this at once raises the question of what sort of virtues and vices these are: what it is, in education, that is in such short supply on the one hand, or that is particularly destructive on the other. Are we, for instance, talking about enthusiasm and apathy, or will-power and laziness, or knowledge and ignorance, or what?

Obviously there is no simple answer to this, because the practice of education at least is partly dependent on local conditions: in some societies, for instance, the inhibiting factors may be simply lack of time and money, or illiteracy, or disease, or civil war. However, my claim is that the virtues and vices most relevant — certainly to our own and other reasonably well-off societies, and I think ultimately to all — are those that might be described as falling within the realm of mental health: marked, perhaps, by such terms as 'seriousness' and 'sophisticated common sense' on the one hand, and 'doctrinaire outlooks', 'partisan feeling' and 'fantasy' on the other. In particular, I have suggested elsewhere (and indeed the general point will seem obvious to many people) that when things go badly wrong in education the chief cause is not ignorance, or lack of empirical research, or practical incompetence, or shortage of resources, but the operation of some powerful (and often unconscious) fantasy that prevents us from approaching the subject seriously and from using our common sense (J. Wilson, 1975). If this is anywhere near the truth, then it needs to be shown not only *that* fantasy does in fact operate in this general way, but also *how* and *where* it operates: what particular fantasies dominate or infest what particular areas.

We may pursue a bit further the question of why and how education is peculiarly liable to the corruption of fantasy, if only because this may illuminate certain general temptations against which we may be on our guard. There are perhaps two reasons amongst others whose joint operation is extremely powerful:

(1) First, education invites us to fantasies of perfection, or at least of changing the (human) world in some rather dramatic way for the better. Of course other enterprises compete with education in this respect, notably religion and politics (or more broadly, 'ideology'); and it is clear that educational theory often tends to be tacked on to some ideology or other as a kind of addendum, rather than being taken seriously as an enterprise in its own right (J. Wilson, 1979). But even if it is taken seriously (and taken out of the more obvious ideological or political hands), education still has a special appeal for those who see the key to progress as some kind of change in the individual mind (rather than in 'society' or 'the system'), and a change effected by *learning* rather than by some other process (conversion, indoctrination, revolution or political control). Thus, insofar as education is, in fact, regarded at least to some extent as a *sui generis* enterprise, its appeal is likely to be especially strong for what may roughly be called liberal ideologists: those who feel that the encouragement of truth-seeking, 'enlightenment', 'critical thinking', 'awareness', 'autonomy', and (perhaps) a broad-based humanism and rationalism will dispel present gloom or strike off existing fetters. The Renaissance humanists, Rousseau, Locke, Dewey, J. S. Mill and Bertrand Russell are obvious examples amongst many. Such thinkers are apt always to neglect or underestimate the kind of difficulties in human nature stressed by more pessimistic writers (Plato, Augustine, Freud). Against such a background it is perhaps less surprising to observe (as we shall observe in this book) the variety of what we may call liberal or left-wing fantasies that imply the possibility of abolishing features of

human and social life that are, in reality, inexpellable: such features as punishment, rules, class distinctions and human differences in general, 'extrinsic motivation' (particularly from fear), and so forth.

(2) The second reason is a more obviously practical one: that in the theory and practice of education the real world does not hit us hard enough or immediately enough, if and when we get things wrong, to jerk us out of our fantasies. Certainly bad education *does* lead to disasters, but not so overtly as bad medicine or bad economics: nobody dies on the operating table or goes bankrupt. Education-alists can get away, and have often got away, with theories and practices that are obviously absurd; with dreams and compulsions that they act out on children. The comparative impotence of children is an important feature here: they are at the receiving end of fantasies whose constituents range from baby-battering and constant beatings to total permissiveness and indiscipline. This point has, of course, less force when what children learn is largely governed by economic or military necessity; but, by the same token, education in such contexts is not much more than elementary socialisation plus a limited amount of vocational training. The fantasies creep in when we have the time and the money to give the enterprise a more substantial backing.

The question now arises of how fantasy is to be dealt with and what expertise is required to deal with it. For clearly, if progress is to be made, we need to identify these fantasies, observe their operation in some detail and be on our guard against them. Philosophy at least is required here, because whatever else we need to know we certainly need to know that some picture, or outlook or set of ideas actually *is* based on or consists of fantasy, rather than being rational or reality-based. By 'philosophy' I shall mean very roughly, the discipline that aims at exhibiting conceptual truths and distinctions and demon-strating conceptual incoherence or muddle; not, of course, 'a philosophy of life' or *Weltanschauung* (something that may itself consist largely of a fantasy picture; see chapter 2). We should not require this particular discipline if education were centrally concerned with empirical facts or propositions whose verification is non-controversial or beyond dispute; we should simply need those sciences or bodies of empirical knowledge that would show up the falsity of certain opinions. But this is not always, nor (I think) even often, the difficulty with education: the difficulty is rather that things go logically or conceptually astray, and that the conceptual incoherence stems from some fantasy or other that has obviated common sense. The philosopher is needed to exhibit the incoherence. To take a parallel: If Nazis or aristocrats had believed, in a straightforward empirical way, that 'Aryan blood' or 'blue blood' was materially different from other kinds of blood, both they and we could have referred the question to biologists or other scientists, to be settled by the normal processes of scientific enquiry. But this was not the kind of belief or picture or outlook that they actually had: the initial difficulty was to make *sense* of their views and to show that — on some interpretations at least — the views were incoherent.

Rather more difficult is the question of how to link the philosophical appreciation of what can and what cannot intelligibly be said with some understanding of the reasons or mental causes that dispose people to say it. Philosophers of a purist disposition might take the view that these are two different tasks, assigning the former to 'philosophy' (or 'conceptual analysis') and the latter to some mixture of empirical disciplines (perhaps psychiatry in particular). But this seems over-simple. For until what is said reaches the point of being *obviously* coherent and intelligible on the one hand, or obviously incoherent and self-contradictory on the other — and at this point the philosopher might cease to be interested — the work consists of trying to *make sense* of what is said; and the notion marked by 'making sense', whatever else it may imply, certainly implies taking into account the intentions of the speaker. It is, primarily, *men* who mean things *by* words: no serious philosopher can be content with glaring at the words by themselves. But once we bring in the idea of the speaker's intentions, it seems hard to set any clear limit of this kind on philosophical enquiry: it is precisely because his intentions are *not* clear (even to himself) that the enquiry is set in motion. He feels something and wants to say something, and the enquiry undertakes to marry what he feels with what can coherently and clearly be said; but how can this be successfully done if one of the marriage-partners is considered irrelevant?

Thus in the early days of positivism it seemed possible for reputable philosophers to dismiss certain things said as 'meaningless':* a

---

*As for instance in A. J. Ayer's *Language, Truth and Logic*, one of the most popular and influential books of that period. Ayer took this line with moral and religious propositions.

possibility only made plausible by straitjacketing the use of language into one or two acceptable postures (notably the scientific posture). Nowadays, partly under the influence of Wittgenstein, we should be more inclined to treat whatever is said with more respect, and consider it against the background or the 'form of life' in which the words are used. But how can this be done except by understanding the feelings that form an essential part of that background? As with intentional action generally, the question of *what* a man wants to say cannot be wholly divorced from the question of *why* he wants to say it. *Pace* any out-and-out relativists (and certain forms of relativism bear, in my judgement, most of the marks of fantasy), we have to acknowledge that there is such a thing as contradiction or logical incoherence; but when that has been established in the case of some particular story, the important work has only just begun. For clearly the person *wants to say something*; and what he wants to say cannot itself be incoherent, for that would be to say nothing. What he actually says may take the form of 'A and not-A'; but that is because he fails to do himself justice, which is in turn due to his not *knowing* what he wants to say, being left only with a (justifiable) feeling of dissatisfaction when the incoherence of what he actually says is pointed out by some philosopher.

But be that as it may: anyone who has attempted to get people to think seriously about educational problems can hardly have failed to notice at least some of the fantasies that make progress very difficult. Philosophy of education must surely take account of this (very obvious) fact. Either we shall disconnect such philosophy from the person's genuine beliefs and feelings, making it into something too sophisticated and, as it were, high-minded for it actually to affect the person's daily thought and practice in education — something kept only for the seminars and tutorials and essays that the regulations demand; or else we attempt to connect philosophy with the student's feelings, which inevitably means making him aware of what those feelings are.

There is also a severely practical point. To become aware of one's fantasies, even in the way I have described — or better still, if one has the time, motivation, money and good luck, by going in for some rather more serious psychotherapy — is often a much *quicker* way of arriving at certain kinds of truth than via surface-level philosophical argument and/or empirical investigation. I say 'often' and 'certain kinds of truth', because obviously a lot depends on how the person concerned stands in his attitude towards this or that form of enquiry; and this depends on a great many factors — not only the inherent difficulties of the enquiry, nor only on his own personality, but also on his social and historical position. Thus as a generalisation it is no doubt true that enquiries roughly to be entitled 'philosophical' or 'psychological' — and much of what comes under 'education' is of this sort — are more liable to fantasy than, say, physics or medicine or geography; yet we have only to think of the way in which these subjects, in many earlier ages, were fantasy-ridden because of the lack of those socially established and institutionalised structures that now defend us, if with some fragility, against fantasy.

To take a central example; if a person can gain some genuine insight into and control over his fantasies about authority, this is likely to improve the rationality of his views and his practice over a wide area of educational topics that are bound up with the notion of authority — discipline, punishment, 'standards', learning, the serious study of curricular subjects, examinations, and so forth — and to improve them much more quickly, and with much less chance of regression or backsliding, than prolonged intellectual discussion. Of course he may be the sort of person to whom intellectual discussion is 'real' — that is, someone who uses it as a method of challenging his own fantasies and prejudices, someone who is prepared for it to *hurt,* and is so much in love with truth that it becomes for him an effective method of change. But such exceptions are rare; nor do I think that intellectual sophistication or public academic performance correlate very much, if at all, with such desirable qualities. There are plenty of highly graded intellectuals to whom such enquiries are no more than games: being intelligent, flexible and imitative, they pick them up quickly, do well at them and lay them aside when they no longer serve some external end (such as getting a good degree).

It is no criticism of philosophy (if 'philosophy' be taken as the title of an enterprise that simply demonstrates conceptual truths and conceptual incoherence) to say that it cannot do much by itself to change the nature of our educational thinking. Nor is this just because (though there is an important truth here) those who are firmly wedded to some fantasy will not even listen to what philosophers have to say; or, if they listen, will not understand it; or, if they understand, will not inwardly digest. It is also because any such change demands two other requirements. First, it is necessary that a person understand not only that he is conceptually incoherent or the victim of fantasy, but also *why* he is. He must realise, that is, what he really wants to say and what purpose his fantasy serves: in particular, perhaps, what he is frightened of and trying to defend himself against. Second, he needs not just to see the error of his ways, but also to see and appreciate certain goods that, if only he could grasp them, would make the incoherence and fantasy unnecessary: one might say, the real goods for which he substitutes apparent goods. Unless these two conditions are met, fantasies behave like the Hydra or like nature: cut off one head, and another grows; expel one symptom, and the disease returns in another form.

I will give two brief illustrations of this point, one from what might be called 'philosophy' and another from 'psychotherapy' — though they should also illustrate something of the uncertainty of, and overlap between, these titles.

(1) An 'anarchist', or somebody who talks as if he regarded all rules as restrictive and unnecessary, can usually be shown up as incoherent: he needs the rules of linguistic usage to formulate an intelligible position, social rules to prevent the kind of authority he dislikes, and so forth (see J. Wilson, 1977, ch. 4). But he needs also to see (a) just what sort of rules and authority he really hates, and whence that hatred stems (from somewhere in his own past history — that, I think, is a necessary truth), and (b) that, as well as restricting, rules also *enable* — that rules have a good (attractive, desirable) aspect. If he does not, he may stop calling himself an 'anarchist' or using certain other words (to avoid the ignominy of apparent self-contradiction, if indeed he regards that as ignominious), but his basic position, his psychic stance (so to speak), will remain the same; and if he talks at all, this stance will continue to emerge in his talk as well as in his other behaviour. On the other hand, once he can see and feel and get used to *some* rules as good, in imagination and practice as well as in philosophical conversation, coupled with some understanding of what aspect of rules he is frightened of, real change is possible.

(2) A person may talk, feel and act as if he wanted both (i) to be totally joined or united to another person (because he is frightened of being separate) and (ii) to be totally free (because he is frightened of being overwhelmed or submerged). These are clearly contradictory, and the person himself can see that they are. But he needs (a) to grasp something of the original childhood situation that

generated these fears and to compare it with his actual position in a grown-up world, and (b) to have some actual experience of feeling himself loved or valued in relation to another person who is neither totally united to nor totally separate from him, if he is to make any real advance. And of course, precisely because of the state he is in, he will *resist* this knowledge and experience fiercely and doggedly, complaining now about his separateness and now about his being smothered. That is why psychotherapy takes a long time and requires the expertise of someone who both understands what sort of game the patient is playing and can encourage him to play a more profitable game instead. Without this he cannot really know (except on paper, as it were) what a proper adult relationship is like; he will simply go on playing his incoherent game with one person after another.

Just as it is possible to hold a doctrinaire position about the teaching of philosophy (or at least, of philosophy of education), so one might also claim that the interaction that might be called 'psychotherapy' can only be effectively conducted in one form. Purist psychoanalysts might insist on a minimum of four or five sessions a week on the couch, for instance, and dismiss much of what other people do by way of 'psychotherapy' as irrelevant or corrupt or at best superficial. Yet there are not only professional but less stringent psychotherapists, but a whole host of other people — counsellors, group leaders, housemasters, tutors, social workers and personal friends, for instance — who may perform effectively, at different levels and in different ways. For pedagogic purposes it may be helpful to say, somewhat dramatically, that we are moving in an area bounded at one end by the strictly philosophical discussion common in high-level philosophy seminars or tutorials, and at the other by the professional Harley Street psychoanalyst; but this middle ground is in no way discreditable.

It becomes discreditable only when (as does, indeed, happen only too often) we fail to make and enforce those distinctions that we *can* make and enforce. The most obvious and important of these is between a form of interaction in which the goal is to determine the truth about some external topic (as in philosophy and most well-established empirical enquiries) and a form in which we aim to find out about, and perhaps learn to control, our own conscious and unconscious emotions. And just as further distinctions can be made within the former area between different kinds of enquiry, so they can be made — though with more difficulty — within the latter: it is, surely, one thing to study emotions in general, another thing to look at one's own emotions (with some distinction or sliding scale between conscious and unconscious emotions), another thing again to acquire the power to change them, and so forth.

Such distinctions are difficult to make even in theory (see J. Wilson, 1971, App. VI, pp. 241ff.); and in practice the position is still more complex, inasmuch as it is not *obviously* true that the right way to proceed is first to sort out and specify different forms of interaction, and then to use only one form at a time. It seems likely — though even this may be going too far — that the learners will profit from understanding the differences between the kinds of games that can be played; but it does not follow that each game should be, as it were, time-tabled and preserved from interference. Some degree of inter-weaving might work better, or work better for some people: an hour in which, for instance, a philosophical enquiry into (say) authority is occasionally allowed to stray towards a more personal enquiry into the feelings of those present. Tidy-minded philosophers are likely to find this unsatisfactory and confusing (I confess to this feeling myself); but that does not prove its inefficiency.

Both the question and the answer turn largely here, I think, on how the learning-group is set up in the first place. If some one person or at most two people are responsible for teaching or guidance in the whole of this area — that is, roughly, both for philosophical enquiry and for emotional awareness — then they will best be able to make the relevant decisions: decisions that, in the nature of the enterprise, will often be *ad hoc* and vary according to the nature of the group. To ask the question in bureaucratic or administrative terms — how many man-hours on 'philosophy', how many on 'emotional aware-ness', etc. — is to go wrong from the start. My own guess (speaking now purely from my own experience of such groups) is that the various tasks do, indeed, require very different contexts. In particular many people — even mature students — are quite inexperienced in *any* kind of even semi-sophisticated group activity; and these have to be led into it gently, building up trust by means of simple corporate or collective activities that pose fewer threats (camping together, playing some game, having a party and so forth). This alone makes it absurd to throw them in at the deep end of 'philosophy' or 'psychotherapy'; the basis of trust and togetherness is just not there, and this basis often takes a great deal of time to establish.

In a way that runs parallel to the above, it is equally absurd to pretend either (i) that we can totally root out or get free from our fantasies, or (ii) that they are so deeply and unconsciously embedded as to make any serious progress impossible. Things stand here as they do in other aspects of moral virtue or mental health: most of us — that is, those who have not given up the struggle altogether — fight some sort of running battle with our fantasies and with the vices that are largely their by-product. We become, perhaps, a little more or a little less aware of them and able to control them: we do not suddenly acquire or relinquish a strong ego. What we can acquire and relinquish in a fairly short space of time, however, is the *idea* of fighting this battle: we may acknowledge our deficiencies and become at least embryonically committed to overcoming them. Notions marked by 'repentance' and 'conversion' may have a place here, however melodramatic or partisan a use may have been made of them by past and present sectarians.

Some distinction must be drawn between those fantasies that are sustained simply by *ignorance* of the truth on the one hand, and those sustained *against* or in the teeth of the truth on the other. This distinction is often not easy to draw, because it is often hard to say whether a man's state is one of sheer ignorance and simple unawareness, or one of more or less consciously embattled defiance: whether he just does not know, or whether he knows but rejects the knowledge by some process of self-deception, hypocrisy or overt bloody-mindedness. It would be convenient to say, as Socrates seems to have done, that 'real' or 'true' knowledge is necessarily overriding; or, as Hare seems to do, that 'sincere' or 'whole-hearted' assent necessarily implies some kind of action (J. Wilson, 1971, pp. 135-9, with references). But apart from other objections (e.g. that one may be all the more sincere or serious about what one preaches precisely because one does *not* practise it: as with errant fathers talking to their sons), this glosses over a wide variety of cases in which the appropriate picture is rejected for very different reasons. 'He would hold this picture steady and act on it if only (a) he stopped to think about it, (b) he realised just how important it was, (c) he understood how he was defending himself against it, (d) he understood why he was defending himself against it, (e) he was given more practice, (f) he could share it with someone else. . .', and so on. These and other kinds of conditions are very numerous, and no serious effort (that I am aware of) has been made to categorise them properly.

Nevertheless we can see at least some of the evasions or defences at work (only rarely, in my judgement, can they fairly be described as 'weakness of will' — however we construe 'will', it is the wrong word). It is rarely a lack of *determination*, or 'will-power': natural terms to use if, say, one is trying to give up smoking. On the contrary: men usually put plenty of power and determination into sustaining and acting out some picture, only it is the wrong picture. (It was not will-power that Hitler lacked). Human desires and emotions go somewhere, and are acted out on some stage. Admittedly they may be locked in internal conflict and thus create the impression of weakness or even non-existence, but this impression is illusory; and in most cases, anyway, the acting-out is evident enough and the stage sufficiently public. The trouble is rather that the drama is inappropriate.

What (it might be asked) is the merit of concentrating, in an apparently negative sort of way, on the vices rather than the virtues? One answer to this, so far as this book is concerned, is to deny the charge: for most of our time will be taken up in showing what the common-sense, rational attitude to certain issues in education actually looks like — that is, in exhibiting the conceptual truths that apply to these issues. For apart from the need already mentioned — that is, to show that the fantasies *are* fantasies — it is not possible to see the fantasies for what they are except in the light of what is true. We shall, in fact, be sometimes outlining a number of necessary truths in a fairly strict philosophical way, so that one can see how it is that fantasy has crept in and obscured them. So there it cannot be said that we are concentrating unduly on the vices.

But it would be disingenuous to rely solely on that reply. I have argued elsewhere, and shall assume here, that in certain departments of life (of which education is one) human beings inevitably — that is, for conceptual or at least profound and immutable empirical reasons — suffer from certain types of mental distortion and from the lack of seriousness (J. Wilson, 1979). We stand in need of something more like a cure or a means to salvation than like a new technique or an improved scientific theory. An objection to concentrating on our defects would be like an objection to doctors concentrating on a patient's diseases; it is only by such concentration that health becomes possible. And (to consider the parallel again) just as the therapist spends his time in freeing the neurotic or the obsessed person from his compulsions so that he can thereafter face the real world with rationality and love on his own, rather than trying to inject him, as it were, with these virtues in some *a priori* way, so (I believe) we need first to free ourselves from the distortions and compulsions that make rational thought impossible; we can then come to see what is sensible and sane without too much difficulty for ourselves.

Finally, some clear, though necessarily brief, account is owed the reader of what I have in mind by the term 'fantasy'. There is no space here for a full deployment of traditional philosophical procedures, involving an investigation of the 'normal use' of the word, 'model' or 'paradigmatic' cases of it, and so forth. Nor, in fact, are such procedures particularly helpful in this instance. 'Fantasy' is not, or not obviously, a term that often functions in 'normal usage' at all, if we are thinking of the common-or-garden, everyday conversations that people have with each other; and it has certainly been taken over, at least partly, by groups with particular interests — psychotherapists, or teachers of English who are interested in 'creativity', for instance — and used (albeit unclearly) as a term of art. (One might compare such terms as 'inferiority complex', 'neurotic', 'role', and many others). It will be easier and clearer if I simply stipulate — though without, I hope the element of arbitrariness that 'stipulate' implies; the stipulation is, so far as I can see, pretty well in accordance with the way in which many contemporary English-speakers use the word.

(1) 'Fantasy', as against such terms as 'illusion', 'delusion', 'prejudice', 'bias' and others, suggests more than a *simple* product of the imagination: something more complex than to suppose a bush a bear, or to see an imaginary dagger, or to feel irrationally hostile to Jews. It suggests something like a story or picture with *connected* elements: for instance, the Nazi story or picture painted in terms of 'Aryan blood', the Führerprinzip, and so on, of which anti-Jewish feeling is only one feature, connected with the others. Similarly a fantasy about blacks might include such elements as 'They're closer to the apes', 'They're more sexually potent', 'They don't feel pain like we do', and so forth: elements bound together in some sort of psychological web.

(2) As against such terms as 'ideal' or 'theory', 'fantasy' suggests that

the story or picture is generated not by concern for truth or fact or any sort of appropriateness to the world, but by the emotional needs of the person in question. Exactly what words may be used here is, again, not easy to settle by any appeal to 'normal usage'. Many terms, as perhaps 'ideology' or '*Weltanschauung*' ('world-outlook'), may be neutral as between emotion-generated and truth-oriented enterprises; one might be prepared to grant that something is an 'ideology' and *also* a 'fantasy', as in the case of Nazi doctrines. But many other terms might be withdrawn once one is convinced that the picture is not really any kind of attempt on truth: the extreme paranoid, we might say, does not really have a *theory* (or even perhaps a set of *beliefs*) that everyone is against him, plotting behind his back, etc.

(3) I do not take it as a defining characteristic of a fantasy that it is false to fact, or inappropriate: it may be, as it were, true *per accidens* (if the person's emotional needs and pictures happen to fit the world). But there is a fairly large class of fantasies, commonly entertained by many people, of which we can say not that they are, empirically, false to fact, but rather that they are conceptually incoherent or logically impossible: that they are of necessity false or inappropriate. It is difficult to give brief and clear examples, because everything turns on how particular words are used. But we can recognise, for instance, how the common fantasy of being totally joined or united to another person may run up against logical difficulties: I cannot have your headache, nor can I be you whilst still remaining me. Similarly the sadist may both want his victims to remain free (so that he can enjoy subjugating them) and also want them to be totally controlled or subjugated; and these wants may not square logically with each other.

There is of course a great deal more that could, and perhaps should, be said here about the nature of fantasies in general; but I plead shortage of space, and a rather more direct practical intent than one might find in, for instance, a philosophical or psychiatric work that discusses the topic in its own right. I shall proceed to consider, first, what philosophy can in principle do to arm us against fantasy; then what seem to me to be the two major fantasies that, in practice, beset educational theory and practice.

CHAPTER 2

What Philosophy Is

We have to start by looking at this topic because we need to see the force of the philosophical procedures we shall be using in this book. These procedures are, I think, fairly well known and well documented; and I do not want to conduct a very lengthy and elaborate defence of them here. But we need to understand roughly what they are, and something of the temptations that lead to abandoning or denying them.

Perhaps we can avoid some of our initial prejudices by taking a science-fiction type example. Suppose we had a visitor from Arcturus who told us that he and his fellows put a lot of time and effort into an activity called, in his language, 'squmping'; and who wanted some advice on how that activity could best be conducted. We should have to say to him something like: 'Well, first of all you'll have to tell us what "squmping" means, otherwise we can't even start. What counts as "squmping", as opposed to doing something else? What are its defining characteristics? And since you put a lot of time and effort into it, what kinds of benefit do you hope to achieve? What counts as a good squmper — is it a matter of technique, or skill, or having your heart in the right place, or being strong, or being brave, or what? Tell us what the activity *is*, and then at least we shall know what to look at.'

Philosophy starts from this (essentially Socratic) notion; and it might be said, not without truth, that it ends there also. Certainly *if* (but it is a big 'if') this kind of clarity, clarity about the meanings and implications of words, is pursued with sufficient ruthlessness and enthusiasm, we may be able to gain all the ground that is necessary. But it is not obvious, in advance and to those who have not practised a good deal of philosophy, what sort of gains these are; and for that reason it may be worth raising in somewhat more detail here the very general questions 'What is philosophy?' and 'What sort of powers or importance does it have?' These are time-honoured questions, raised by Plato and many other philosophers since Plato. My excuse for raising them with such brevity here is that we have (in my judgement) reached, or nearly reached, a position from which we can give one or two clear answers.

Philosophical truth

If we want to know — putting it bluntly — what use or good philosophers are, we shall best interpret the question 'What is philosophy?' along the lines of 'What *kind* of truth, and what kind of arguments for it, do philosophers uniquely dispense?' or 'How do philosophers distinguish themselves as truth-finders as against, say, historians or scientists or literary critics or psychologists?'

Outside the Anglo-Saxon tradition in philosophy — the tradition that distinguishes 'philosophy' from the erection or sale of certain 'philosophies' or 'philosophies of life' — this question seems to me very hard to answer. Various outlooks, 'world-views', creeds, 'faiths to live by', etc. are produced, to which we may be more or less attracted; but even when it is clear that these are *supposed* to be true (rather than just appealing, or beautiful, or moving, or politically effective), it is not clear *how* they are supposed to be true: that is, what kinds of arguments or evidence they are based on. Do they rely on some kind of facts, and if so what kind? Also, if so, are not these facts already wielded by some other expert? Thus if Marxism — assuming, what is untrue, that we know just what to put under that heading — is supposed to rest on historical or economic facts, presumably it must be some kind of historical or economic theory; but then why call it *philosophy*? Do they rely on pure logic? But then it is not easy to see (a) how pure logic can produce outlooks and creeds of such a substantive and detailed kind, or (b) why these outlooks and creeds should be so diverse and often mutually contradictory.

Within the Anglo-Saxon tradition, and more particularly within the way of doing philosophy (or of conceiving philosophy) that has grown up in the UK, the Commonwealth countries, the USA and elsewhere in the last fifty years or so, the question is more easily answerable. Philosophers are supposed to deal in what are called 'conceptual' truths. These are, if you like, truths of logic; but not of formal logic. The idea is that certain concepts, marked of course by certain words in natural languages, are logically related to others in various ways. Often — as with the simple examples that we usually rely on — these relations are very obvious: triangles must (logically) have three sides, bachelors must be unmarried, and so on. In a slightly less obvious way, the concept marked by (say) 'learn' may be seen to imply some idea of mastering something and of attending to certain standards; that marked by 'discipline' to imply some idea of obedience to an established authority; that marked by 'society' or 'social communication' to imply some notion of a norm of truth-telling. The philosopher's business, it is believed, is to exhibit these conceptual (or 'logical' or 'linguistic') relationships: to show what can be said — in any language, not just English — with consistency and coherency and intelligibility, and what cannot.

This well-known approach to philosophy (or persuasive definition of 'philosophy'), sometimes called 'Oxford philosophy', 'linguistic analysis', 'analytic philosophy' or (by J. L. Austin, one of its most powerful practitioners) 'linguistic phenomenology', has thus gained ground by making us clearer about a particular or *sui generis* activity (fairly termed 'philosophy', though that does not matter much) with its own set of procedures, its own type of truth and its own standards of evidence. Instead of producing large-scale outlooks, ways of life or sets of values in a way reminiscent of sages or super-scientists, the philosopher is to be found properly at home with *one* particular type of truth, variously called 'linguistic truths', 'logical truths', 'conceptual necessities', 'analytic truths', and so on. These truths are reached by considering, first, what *words* mean and imply (usually in English, since this brand of philosophy is wielded mostly by English-speakers, but nothing prevents the same procedure being followed in French or any other language), and second, what *concepts* are and imply.

The former leads to the latter. We start perhaps with a word, 'authority', and note that, as used in English, the meaning of this word has various implications: most obviously perhaps, the idea of being accepted as having or deserving to have some kind of legitimate power or influence. So far this is a truth merely about the meaning of the English word. However, we can then say that *if* there are, or were, words in other languages that meant the same, then (of course) they would have the same implications; and there might actually be such words. Then, instead of mentioning all these words in various languages, we might want to talk about the *concept* marked (in English) by 'authority', or as people sometimes loosely say, 'the concept of authority'. We are interested in the logical implications contained in a certain package, which happens to be marked by 'authority' in English, but could equally well be marked by any sign.

It is, of course, in an obvious sense a matter of *fact* whether a certain word has a certain meaning or set of implications; and one can get some way in finding this sort of thing out by using a good dictionary. But not always very far: for we are not always conscious of the rules of use for words, even though we may use them correctly. We have to unearth these rules (learned unconsciously when we were very young) and make them conscious. Asked what the rules are on the spot, we are likely to give an inadequate reply — as Socrates' victims do in almost every Platonic dialogue. Such replies can be tested by seeing what, in various cases, we actually could or could not intelligibly say: what would be self-contradictory and what would make perfectly good sense. The philosopher is supposed to be the expert in this process of unearthing and testing out.

The ultimate weapon, so to speak, of philosophy as thus described is the notion of contradiction. If someone said, for instance, 'Human beings should have no rules when dealing with each other', the philosopher would try to show that this was internally incoherent or contradictory, that there was something logically contained in the idea, or concept, of human interaction (as against, say, billiard balls bumping into each other) that itself implied the existence of rules: for instance, the rules of language that are usually obeyed when people talk to each other and that alone make communication possible. The philosopher simply (!) shows what is implied by what one says, when one takes time off to think properly about it: 'If you say A, then that means you have to say B as well, but that you can't coherently say C', and so on.

The powers of philosophical truth

I think — no, I am quite sure — that this account leaves many people feeling dissatisfied. The philosopher can certainly show that failure to philosophise — failure to attend to the conceptual implications of what one says — may lead not only to muddle and incoherence, but to great danger. For instance, if Germans around the 1930s had thought seriously and philosophically about notions marked by 'Aryan blood', 'sub-men', 'racial purity' and so on, it is possible that a lot of bloodshed would have been averted. This is not just a question of being linguistically tidy, of 'defining one's terms' in order to be intellectually respectable; it is a matter of needing to get clear in order to avert the pressures of fantasy and prejudice, which operate disastrously in the real world when we fail to inspect and check them.

However, this is an essentially negative or therapeutic power — though none the less important for that. On this account — so far as we have taken it, at least — the philosopher cannot tell you any important truths *about the world* in a positive sort of way. All he can do (though this is plenty, and alone would justify philosophy) is to prevent you getting into a muddle and allowing your prejudices and fantasies to emerge unchecked into speech and action. For (the story goes) the philosopher deals, as we have seen, only with conceptual (logical) truths, not with matters of fact; these he leaves to the scientist, or the historian, or to whoever it may be that deals with particular kinds of fact.

A good, and perhaps central, example of this can be found in moral or political philosophy. The story might be something like this: 'Different people have different political or moral values: they talk about, and justify what they do under such terms as, "love" or "democracy" or "justice" or whatever. Some people admire one sort of system, others another sort. Now the philosopher can help by making these (very different) views internally consistent. He can tell you what the concepts you use in spelling out your view imply, and what they cannot imply. If you talk of "justice", and mean what you say, then such-and-such follows, and so-and-so cannot follow. But what the philosopher cannot do is to tell you what concepts to start with, what systems to adopt in the first place. That is a matter for each individual to settle for himself: philosophers are — nowadays at least — not out to proselytise or convert or preach. Once you have got some game going, he can perhaps clarify the rules for you; but he cannot tell you what games to play.'

I think, though I do not know, that something like this is the prevailing orthodoxy today. An excellent example of it may be found in Sir Isaiah Berlin's television broadcast that opened the 'Men of Ideas' series in mid-January of 1978 (available from the BBC, London). In particular, stress is laid on the fact that philosophers do not take sides when it comes to 'substantive' issues, whether of a moral/political nature or not. They do not tell you how the world is, or how it ought to be. Each man must judge this for himself. There is still a very considerable fear of philosophers seeming to be 'experts' in the old-time sense of sages who have some kind of magic insight, denied to the rest of us, in virtue of which they ought to be obeyed.

Part of the reason for this fear may simply be that the prevailing fashion is very much against the idea of 'experts', at least of this kind. It seems undemocratic and anti-egalitarian. Moreover, the kind of people who are attracted to philosophy — in liberal countries where this kind of philosophy is practised — are perhaps more than usually keen on intellectual autonomy: they are good or even paradigmatic liberals, against censorship, in favour of open politics, against anything that smacks of totalitarianism or indoctrination, in favour of autonomy, self-determination and the other liberal virtues. There is, however, still something very fishy about this position.

What is fishy is this. One of two things: either we believe that it is, in a fairly strict sense, *arbitrary* what games we play, what concepts we choose to base our lives on, what moral and political values we assert — in the sense that no good reasons can be given for one or the other set of concepts or values; or we believe, though we may be unclear about how to prove, that things are not arbitrary in this sense — that *there are reasons* for jumping this way or that. I doubt whether anyone seriously believes the former; but if he did, it would be hard to see much value in philosophy. For what would be the *point* of clearing up muddles, exhibiting conceptual implications, producing clarity and consistency and (in general) philosophising, if we did not think that this would help us to choose more *correctly*? Why bother to make the Nazis think about what they say and claim to believe, if this will not put them in a *better* frame of mind than before? On the other hand, if there actually are criteria by which we should make our moral and political judgements — if we can use good or bad reasons in this department of life — then it ought to be the philosopher's business to tell us what they are; and this surely brings in the idea of *some* kind of expertise. The expertise would be that of a person who, whilst not issuing particular orders, nevertheless showed us in a general sort of way what *sort* of orders we should attend to; who gave us a proper understanding of the methodology, as it were, of doing morality or politics or science or history or whatever. And that would be a very important sort of expert indeed.

I believe the latter to be true. The reason I believe it to be true — and the point is independent of the particular examples of morality and politics — is that it seems clearly *not* entirely a matter of individual human choice to determine what concepts we shall start with. As human beings, we are *landed with* a great many concepts that we have to use: 'have to', not because of any empirical compulsion, but because these concepts are a logically inevitable part of the furniture of any conceivable world. Space forbids me to give too many examples; but it seems clear, for instance, that basic categories like space itself, time, cause and effect, the notion of 'good' and 'bad', and the various emotions that are generated by these preconditions, certain implications that must be true of *any* human society (like the norm of truth-telling) and a good many other things are — so to speak — *given*. They are the limits or the necessary furniture not only of our world but of any possible world. And if that is so, it is obviously of great practical importance that everyone should realise it.

The arguments for this would be, appropriately, philosophical or conceptual arguments; not empirical arguments about how the world actually is but conceptual arguments about how any world must be. In practice, we take our point of departure from the notion (into which a good deal is packed) of a conscious creature, Martian or human makes no matter, in a space-time continuum. From these concepts a great many implications follow. Among them, as I believe, would be a large number of things that were, necessarily, advantages or disadvantages for any such creature: 'goods' and 'evils'. (Much of Aristotle's ethics is concerned with these.) If, as I claim, it is *logically* inevitable that any such creature will feel (say) hope and regret — briefly, since there will inevitably be future goods that he anticipates or past mistakes that he observes — then it is no good trying to banish these and other emotions (hope, or fear, or guilt, or anger, or any other) from human life: they are given, though of course we may wish to attach them to different objects.

All this is impossibly sketchy but I hope sufficient to show the line of argument with which I am concerned. The point is that, if this is correct, then there is an important sense in which the people dissatisfied with modern analytic philosophy are quite right. They are wrong if they demand empirical, or pseudo-empirical, truths about life, as it were from sages with X-ray eyes. But they are right if they demand that they should be told some truths about life or about the world, truths of a conceptual kind but that nevertheless have great practical importance.

Nor does this abrogate their freedom. It is not an abrogation of freedom that one has to obey the law of non-contradiction in order to say anything intelligible; and other conceptual truths about the (or any) world are not compulsions or empirical limits. We have the choice between accepting and understanding them on the one hand, or failing to grasp them and allowing our irrational fantasies free play on the other. It is here, I think, that the problems of philosophy come in: we naturally entertain a strong feeling of resistance to any kind of truth that denies our impulses or fantasies. This resistance is common both to what I earlier called the negative or therapeutic function of philosophy (to clear up muddle) and to the more positive function that I have (too briefly) tried to describe.

One thing at least is plain. There *is* such a thing as (in the words of the Philosophy Society's motto) 'wisdom to direct' and 'knowledge to govern'. It is *not* the case that — putting it briefly — there are empirical truths but after that it is each man for himself. We have to hang tightly on to what has been gained by the modern analytic movement in philosophy: not just to the importance of clarity and precision, but to the point that the philosopher deals in a certain kind of truth, conceptual truth. These gains are not slender. We must not regress to the painting of world-pictures of a vague and generalised kind, which are in any case more likely to be the product of our own fantasies than of anything else. Perhaps the most important thing is to get as many people as possible to understand what philosophy is; to engage in philosophical discussion; to grasp what truth, evidence and proof in philosophy look like. Then they, and we, can consider just what force this sort of truth has for practical living.

Failure to grasp this more positive aspect of philosophy may account for the gulf between philosophy of education and practical education. It must, I think, be admitted that 'gulf' is not too dramatic a word. Granted that philosophy may often exercise its beneficent influence in unseen and undramatic ways, nevertheless to all appearances its effect on educational theory and practice has been minimal. I am still talking, of course, about 'philosophy' in the sense in which that term is normally understood in most English-speaking countries today and for the last fifty years or so, not about 'philosophies' ('ideologies') of education; not, indeed, that I believe the latter to be in themselves causally effective, since most seem to be not much more than rationalisations of attitudes that would affect theory and practice in any case, i.e. even without the intellectualised top-dressing. Nor do I imply that certain philosophers, in the modern sense, may not have exercised considerable influence: Dewey and Russell are perhaps cases in point. I mean rather that the kind of truth, evidence and argument that are peculiar to philosophy and that may be briefly marked by such terms as 'conceptual' or 'logical' have not much affected the practical scene.

By 'the practical scene' I include not only what goes on in the classroom, but also (what is perhaps a bit more surprising) the whole apparatus of educational theory and educational research. This apparatus has grown considerably in the last few decades: the time, money and manpower expended on it now constitute in many countries a major industry. Generally speaking, however, the industry is manned and managed by non-philosophers: for the most part by sociologists, psychologists and others. Even at the theoretical level the part played by philosophy is very small. In consequence, since it seems that educational fashion is influenced by educational theory, it is unsurprising that practising teachers as well as administrators and theorists remain largely untouched by conceptual and logical insight.

On some of the disastrous consequences of this I have remarked elsewhere (J. Wilson, 1975); but our failure is all the more striking in that we have recently seen able philosophers who have devoted an immense amount of time and effort not only to the subject itself but to bridging this gulf (one has only to think of Professor Peters). Their work must, indeed, have made the subject more intellectually respectable and of more interest to other philosophers, and no doubt also much of what they say sinks into the minds of practical educators (even, perhaps, of administrators and politicians). But how much public effect does it have on educational practice? I say this not to deprecate their work, but simply to show how stiff the opposition must be: our failure, it seems, cannot result only from laziness or lack of ability.

Can anything be said or done, that we are not already saying and doing, to bridge the gulf? It has to be accepted, largely for reasons that I have discussed elsewhere and that have been brilliantly described by Plato in the *Republic,* that there will always be a good deal of built-in opposition to philosophy of any kind, not least in areas such as education that tend to attract an unusual amount of prejudice and fantasy. But part of the trouble is that philosophers underestimate the force of their own discipline. For, as I have briefly suggested, the prevailing view of philosophy amongst philosophers (I exclude those who have, as it seems to me, sold out to sociology and reneged on the whole notion of analytic truth) might be termed Socratic rather than Platonic. I mean, roughly, that philosophy is thought to be of great importance as a means of achieving clarification and consistency; or, negatively, of avoiding muddle and nonsense. It is seen essentially as a critical discipline; and this may be one of the reasons why laymen see it as failing to provide any 'answers' or important truths relevant to practical action. The message that gets across, fairly or unfairly, is that so long as we are clear and careful and accurate, particularly about the meanings of words, anything goes — anything, that is, by way of 'values' or 'ideologies'. Of course there might be a sense in which that message said enough, if we build enough into the notions of 'being clear' and 'the meanings of words'. But, as it stands, it is not sufficient.

I have tried to show why it is not sufficient. First, there are conceptual truths that have immense practical force when combined with certain features of human existence, features that may either themselves be conceptually inevitable and inexpellable or be so deep-rooted empirically as to be fairly regarded as inevitable for all immediate practical purposes. Many of these truths show up more clearly when attached to particular human enterprises, themselves either conceptually or empirically inevitable (like education). Second, it seems that these truths, however obvious some of them may be (and some of them are), fail to receive adequate attention; it is *not* the case that our common sense or sanity or untutored reasonableness keep us so firmly on the right path that we have no need of philosophical backing. Were it always or even usually the case, much of the point of educational philosophy would disappear.

Plato was, I think, right in maintaining (though in a terminology somewhat too metaphysical for the modern taste) that it is essential for at least some people — preferably those in control of affairs — to have a firm philosophical grasp of the essence or form of certain concepts or ideas: that is, to know with as much certainty as is possible why the important conceptual truths are true. For even if common sense and intuitive sanity prevail for a time, which in education rarely happens, they represent too fragile a defence against prejudice and fantasy; a defence that even social fashion may sweep away, and that is only secure when based on adequate reasons. That is why we need to see the conceptual necessity of many things in education that our common sense, when we use it, may vaguely see to be in some weaker sense necessary.

Plato also seems to have rightly maintained that there are *some* enterprises (education is one) where these conceptual truths have a certain priority or pre-eminence: roughly, those in which it is important to see the proper *form* and limits, together with what may be called the conceptual trappings, of what we are engaged in. Otherwise everything goes wrong from the start. It is, then, not just that philosophers 'have something to contribute', or that it is useful to hear 'the philosophical point of view'. Such phrases, at least on some lips, are no more than lip-service to what is — or use to be — a respected and slightly awesome discipline. If philosophers do not have the last word in education and other such enterprises, they ought certainly to have the first.

These claims, which I have tried to explicate in more detail elsewhere (J. Wilson, 1979), are (I suspect) not entirely in harmony with certain features of the modern philosophical temperament. Rightly when confronting other philosophers, but wrongly when confronting the rest of the world, most of us tend to be sceptical and contra-suggestible: seeking, like good Popperians, for some weakness in theses presented by our fellows, or even denying that any such theses are possible. That is, of course, much to be commended both when teaching or learning philosophy and when trying to write it; certainly when compared with magniloquence, ideologising or mere dogmatism. Nevertheless, the impression is conveyed to laymen that there is virtually *nothing* on which philosophers are agreed — nothing, at least, of a positive nature: it is not hard to find philosophers agreeing that such-and-such will *not* do, but much harder to find them agreeing that such-and-such is correct. Indeed, so strong is this impression that one hesitates between saying (a) that there is, in fact, no measure of agreement amongst philosophers at all, and (b) that there is some measure, but that philosophers have not sufficiently clarified and stressed it to the outside world (being, perhaps, bored by what is already settled and anxious to get on to more controversial points).

If, which is much to be hoped, philosophers were to be sufficiently concerned with the improvement of conditions in the practical world to stress — at least on appropriate occasions — the *positive* truths and conceptual necessities with which human beings are landed, they would be able to give educators a much clearer lead. Only so, indeed, can philosophy adequately dispel fantasy; for if the negative aspect alone is stressed, the implication will remain that — putting it briefly — men can respectably maintain whatever world-pictures they like, so long as they are clear and consistent. The facts are, however, that a great deal of the furniture of our world is *given*. What furniture this is — what, as it were, is written into the lease and what is dispensable — is a question that cannot be answered generally: it can only yield to an inspection of particular cases. Some points will, I hope, emerge in the examples that we shall look at later. Here I have attempted only to show why philosophy can, in a very real sense, tell us what the world is (must be) like and what the education of human beings is (must be) like. That, when established and appreciated in detail, is a considerable gain: enough, perhaps, to justify the ancient and ultimately respectable desire for philosophers to be — in this one respect — wiser than the rest of us; or if not wiser, clearer about how the condition of man and the nature of certain human enterprises must necessarily be.

CHAPTER 3

Two Major Fantasies

In describing any fantasies, some important methodological questions arise: how, for instance, and at what level are we to categorise and individuate the items? For it is misleading to speak, as we may seem already to have done, as if there were a number of fantasies that could be discretely and independently identified in some unchallengeable way. Fantasies are organic growths, with a history and a development of their own. Thus in the case of extreme racial prejudice, for instance, we might raise the question of *how many* fantasies prejudiced people were liable to; and this would be hard to answer even by itself (does a fantasy about black people's greater sexual potency, physical strength and 'closeness to the animals' count as one fantasy or two or three?). If we add the notion of different levels, it becomes harder still: is there, for instance, one deep-level fantasy (perhaps fear of sexual domination) that in some sense generates the others?

This topic would repay philosophical and psychiatric study; but for the purposes of this book I shall take a fairly short way through the difficulties. All or most of the mistakes we shall be looking at (which include, as I see it, all or most of the most important ways in which education goes wrong) can be reduced to two basic fantasies, from which other fantasies, pieces of prejudice, doctrinaire practices and types of unreason fairly obviously flow; or — if 'flow' suggests a too severely causal picture — of which they can be seen as illustrations. There is a sense, as we shall see, in which we might reduce these two to one; but that, in my judgement, would be to generalise too much. It would be like giving the empty if sound advice 'Face reality' or 'Don't be a prey to fantasy', when what the patient wants to know is something about *how,* or in *what mode*, he fails to

27

face reality. Some may think that even two is an insufficient number: my hope must be that their variations will become evident when we consider the educational topics that they infest.

We are as apt to fantasise about ourselves, our own minds and natures, as about other things. Education shares with other enterprises (politics, morality, mental health and others) the important feature that its subject matter is concerned with the human *mind*; in particular, with people learning things. It is not concerned, as science is, with the physical world of planets and atoms; or, as mathematics, with a timeless world of logical truths. Even history and the arts are, in this respect, more trouble-free than education: for, though they deal with human intentions and products, they do so within fairly narrow and well-understood limits. It is, in general, now tolerably clear what kinds of questions historians ask and what sort of evidence is required to answer them, though certain sorts of fantasies (notoriously those of a sociological or political kind) are apt to disturb historical enquiry. So too with the arts: although even music and painting, and (more understandably) literature, are liable to be interpreted politically, there exists a strong tradition by which these and other arts are considered in themselves: i.e. by aesthetic criteria. But education requires a sane picture of people as such, and people as learners, in a much more general way: a way that puts education in the front line along with politics and morality and religion, which also require such general pictures.

It is with great difficulty, as many writers have pointed out (Plato and Freud perhaps most vividly), that we tolerate having minds at all. The ego is precarious: created only with great striving and effort, maintained not easily in the teeth of an uncaring and often positively hostile world on the one hand and our passionate non-rational desires on the other. For about eight hours out of twenty-four, it disappears and goes off duty; for much of the rest of the time it may be asleep at its post, leaving the gate open for day-dreaming and other activities to which reason is largely irrelevant. At other times, again, it may be no more than what Hume said it ought to be — the slave of the passions, operating only to gratify its owner, not to advise him on what is for the general good. Unsurprisingly, there is some (often large) part of ourselves that hates and fears it: for it imposes a burden upon us that we undertake usually with reluctance. Being reasonable, prudent, wise, sensible, logical, careful — these

are not things that we (in part) want to be, not things that excite, or arouse, or even comfort us. We pay lip-service to them because we know in our saner moments that they are necessary. But we do not like them.

Unsurprisingly also, this dislike is rationalised. To defend ourselves against the burden of our own minds, we adopt pictures of the mind that allow us to diminish or abolish the burden. Very roughly speaking, we come to see the mind either (a) as not subject to any standards, principles, rules, laws, criteria or rational procedures at all — as if it consisted only of unmediated impulse and feeling, or (b) as subject to the standards or criteria that govern physical objects — as if it were a complicated piece of engineering only, or a kind of computer. Either of these two moves enables us to elude what frightens us: the fact that the human mind (some might say, the soul) is indeed subject to rational criteria, but to criteria more subtle (though no less stringent) than those governing physical objects. Saving and losing one's soul, to put it dramatically, are not like saving or losing money; but one can save it or lose it just the same. There is such a thing as living well and using the mind well, though it is a different sort of thing from investing well; such a thing as being reasonable or mentally healthy or wise, though different from being strong or physically healthy or rich.

I do not think that we are chiefly alarmed by the *intellectual* elusiveness of the criteria that govern the mind or soul, for in fact many of these are not intellectually elusive at all: that is, we do not require a superbly high intelligence or great intellectual sophistication to perceive them. In a sense, we know some of them quite well. We know that love is important, that people matter, that friendship and simple contentment are worth more than riches, and a whole host of other truisms that appear not only in works of religion and philosophy but on tear-off calendars and simple verses in our daily papers. What alarms us is that we only know these things, as Aristotle says, in the way that a drunk man quotes Euripides. They are not *real* to us; if they were, we would behave more in accordance with them.

To say that they are not real is, I think, better than saying (with St Paul and many other writers in that tradition) that we know them perfectly well but fail to *act* on them (through weakness of will, weakness of the flesh, lack of determination or some similar failure in the executive virtues). Of course there are some cases — notably, perhaps, drug addiction — of which this would be a fair description.

But, generally speaking, we do not hold these truths steadily in mind even at the first beginnings of our thought and behaviour. It is, usually, more like falling in love: we do not want to court and marry the girl next door who (we assume here) will make us happy and contented, but find ourselves lacking in the determination or will-power to do so; rather we want, right from the start, to court (if not marry) the girl who takes our fancy. The Nazis did not know that Hitler was a mad tyrant, but found themselves drawn to him like sleep-walkers: they did not *see* him as a mad tyrant. When things go wrong, it is because our whole picture of the world — the concepts we use to see it by — is corrupted right from the start. It is, then, neither lack of intellectual ability nor weakness of will that causes the trouble (unless, of course, we stretch either of those phrases to cover the appropriate ground). It is, precisely, the fact that our fantasies and desires overwhelm us. We lack not intelligence or will-power, but the ability to step back from ourselves, reflect, attend to our own feelings and the world, and hold our attention steady. That ability may correlate with intelligence and will-power, but it is phenomenologically distinct from either; and there are many people to whom we would ascribe both but who do not possess this essential feature.

Most of us are alarmed because we do not have it (or much of it). One way out of this alarm is to hand the problem over to some creed or faith, usually of a religious nature, that will handle it for us. Too often, however, this simply results in our being *told* by some external authority (rather than telling ourselves, which is what we really need) what our position in the world is and how to handle it; moreover, the choice of a faith — though 'choice' is usually too kind a word, since belief of this kind tends to overtake people rather than be rationally reached — is apt itself to be dictated by fantasy. There is of course nothing wrong, and much right, in (as it were) structuring and institutionalising a set of precepts and insights into some clear format, such as a religious creed; but the important thing is that any such creed should be (i) correct, i.e. containing the correct precepts and principles, and (ii) the person's *own*, i.e. something that he himself sees and knows to be correct. The possibility of 'a faith to live by' simply rephrases our basic difficulty.

Against that general background, then, we can identify two major fantasies. I shall call these the Relativist Fantasy and the Behaviourist

Fantasy respectively (RF and BF for short). They are worth slightly more general description than I have yet given them. So far as education is concerned, someone in the grip of the Relativist Fantasy would be likely to fall into that educational (or rather ideological) camp perhaps fairly marked by such terms as 'progressive', 'child-centred', 'egalitarian', 'left-wing' and others. He would be likely to stress 'autonomy' rather than 'standards', and perhaps adopt a Rousseauesque or even Sartrean view of human nature, according to which the individual (or perhaps Nature) in some way makes or creates *his own* 'standards'. The RF tends to go along with an anti-authoritarian attitude: 'Who is to say' — one commonly hears, spoken fairly aggressively, from those in the grip of the RF — 'what counts as right or wrong, good or bad, success or failure, at least in the areas of morality and art and personal relationships?' Much that seems wrong to such people is put down to 'social conditioning', and they tend not to accept non-negotiable differences between people (for instance, between men and women). They are, in general, tender-minded and make much of cultural differences (with the implication that standards are 'relative' or 'subjective').

The Behaviourist Fantasy moves in the other direction. Someone in the grip of the BF will find his educational standards in the standards used by the natural sciences. He will seek — to use an obviously lunatic example — for 'behavioural objectives' even in areas where *behaviour*, in any normal sense of the word, is inappropriate: for instance, in evaluating a person's response to Shakespeare, or his appreciation of Beethoven. Success will be something easily quantified or measured, perhaps something to be reduced to a set of 'skills' or 'performances' or (and the absurdity of the word gives some of the game away) 'behaviours'. He will tend to the tough-minded, 'scientific', even perhaps 'materialistic' style of thinking, being concerned with the 'hard facts' and not with less palpable phenomena.

One way in which the RF emerges is in the idea of a *private world of experience,* governed by private criteria of identification and appropriateness. Since few people, even in educational theory, are mad enough to escape entirely from public criteria in respect of physical objects (those who are do not usually survive), this world is usually restricted to areas where the public criteria are less obvious. Characteristically this is the world of 'the emotions', 'subjective experience', 'personal knowledge', or 'faith'; contraposed, in the RF, to the public world of 'reason', 'objectivity', 'the analytical intelligence' and so forth. The psychological advantages of this are obvious: we preserve at least some part of our lives in an autistic state, free from public authority, rules and standards. We can do what we like with it, structure it as we please (or not at all), call what we like good and bad. If autistic rights over physical objects and other realms have been taken from us by the harsh public taskmasters of science and other disciplines, at least we may keep safe such realms as natural beauty, love, personal relations, art and literature, religion, perhaps even morality. As Milton's Satan says, 'Here at least We shall be free. . . Here we may reign secure; and, in my choice, To reign is worth ambition, though in hell.'

We may talk sanely of a 'private world', just as we may talk of a man's 'private life'. However, though not everything is on show, everything can, at least in principle, be shown: the private world is not free from criteria. If, *per impossibile,* it were so free, it would not be a world of human experience at all — indeed, not a world of experience: there would be no identifiable person to experience. Human consciousness — or, more briefly, consciousness — is always consciousness *of* something, and is necessarily impregnated with language and rules or at least with some criteria of identification. This is not a barrier but an enablement: language does not stand between us and the world, but creates or helps to create the world for us. The only alternative is preconscious infancy, the child asleep at its (not yet his) mother's breast; the innocence of Eden before the knowledge of good and evil; the paradisal or oceanic free floating of a trance or a dream. Such a state appears to many as an immensely attractive alternative to a harsh world, and is ardently pursued in various forms (drugs, meditation, religious doctrines); but it amounts to the suicide of the self. The self is, of necessity, *over against* the world; if it were not, there would be no self and no world.

Just as the RF may push the word 'private' beyond its proper limits in the way, so the BF may narrow and misconstrue the notion marked by 'public'. Such enterprises as science, morality, literature and indeed the practice of language itself, are, in a clear sense, necessarily public: that is, they require the interaction of a number of human beings, and some non-private (non-autistic) checks or verifications of what is said and done. But it does not follow from this that any *particular* group of men, any *particular* 'society' or 'public' defines and adjudicates these enterprises correctly. What is true in science, right in morality, successful in literature, correct in language, is not necessarily the same as what is *thought* (by a particular public) to be true, right, successful or correct. Again, 'sane' does not mean 'what most people think to be sane'; nor are such enterprises as art, religion or education to be identified with particular social practices ('when I say religion of course I mean the Christian religion and when I say the Christian religion of course I mean the Church of England').

To make such identifications — to take 'society' or a 'consensus' as authoritative — is just another way of trying to shrug off the burden of reason and find safety in some fixed and easily identifiable set of rules. In this the BF is like the RF: the one entrusts the business of choice and reason to an external authority ('society', the superego); the other entrusts it to inner impulse ('it's just how you feel', the id). Would that life were so simple: would that we could rely absolutely either on what the neighbours think, or on our unmediated impulses and desires. But the one turns us into ants or robots, and the other into infants or lunatics.

It might be possible to describe a common background to the RF and the BF — whether in the shape of a causal story or merely as a sort of paradigmatic possibility. If you are a young child, and there are people around telling you to 'be good' or 'act rightly', it will be tempting — if one cannot entirely grasp the real *reasons* for what counts as 'good' or 'right' — to jump in one or other of two ways. Either you are contra-suggestible and in some degree reject the authority of those around you; particularly when you notice that different parents and schoolmasters enjoin different things (give 'good' and 'right' a different content), you may be tempted to deny the whole possibility of an 'objective' set of values for which there are objectively valid reasons and talk as if everything were 'just a matter of taste', 'culture-dependent', or whatever — one person's desires and values, as it is often said, are as 'valid' as another's. Alternatively, since you can see the particular overt behaviour that is approved of (even if you cannot see the reasons for it), you may identify 'being good' or 'acting rightly' in a Pharisaic sort of way — that is, with the specific pieces of (as it were) visible or photographable or measurable behaviour, forgetting about the motives, intentions, attitudes and so on that in fact are closely bound up with it.

In this microcosmic description we may recognise some of the roots of the RF and the BF respectively. It is, I think, extremely probable that they stem psychically from some attitude to parental authority, since parental authority is, in fact, a primary and paradigmatic case in which, as a child, one meets the idea of standards, rules and the operation of reason on desire generally. The way in which one receives this is likely to affect one's general attitude to authority, in more subtle senses of that word, in later life: one's attitude, we might say, to what counts (if anything counts) as *getting it right*. This extends far beyond the moral sphere, though perhaps the moral sphere — or the sphere of personal behaviour — is central, if only because it is that which most parents are particularly concerned with. However, I think it would be wrong to claim that the RF and BF stem *solely* from the social interaction of child and parent-figures. For the parents are only one, admittedly very obvious and potent, source of rules and impositions. Life itself — I mean, the fact that the world in general (not only parents) does not yield immediately to one's desires — imposes restraints and limits. The child is faced with the fact that, parents or no, he has to adopt *some* attitude to the harsh realities of the world. He may either try to evade and deny them, or try to get what he wants by conforming to simple, behaviourist rules that may not be sophisticated enough to meet the case: rather as some people open cans and cook things in whatever way they feel like, while others diligently conform to the instructions on the label.

It ought, I think, to be fairly clear (and should emerge when we consider particular examples) that the *same* person may be in the grip of *both* fantasies at different times. Indeed that is very likely to be the case; for one fantasy in a sense compensates for the other. A man may, as it were, unconsciously decide to give his desires more or less free rein in one or two departments of life, whilst maintaining an over-rigid and too mechanistic way of living in other departments; or conduct this slightly schizoid enterprise even within the same department by using different objects — rather as some men will give their sexual desires free rein with their mistresses but control them rigidly with their wives.

This creates additional trouble (as perhaps that example may suggest); for though men have in some sense to make deals with the various parts of themselves, for fear of going mad, they do not always make the wisest deals. By splitting their lives into different areas and assigning each area to a totally independent commander, they lose the value of cooperation and consultation between the commanders. Thus someone who thinks that there is *no* scope in science or chess for creativity, imagination and other virtues governed by fairly 'loose' criteria or standards will not make a very good scientist or chess player; and the same man, if he thinks that the practice of (say) literary criticism or philosophy ought in *no* sense to be 'scientific' (i.e. accurate, 'objective', rigorous, etc.), will not do well at those subjects either.

Such a move occurs again and again in educational theory and practice; and again and again we shall want to remind ourselves, to quote a well-known philosophical maxim, that 'everything is what it is and not another thing': that is, to remind ourselves simply to look at each case *for what it is,* rather than assimilating it to some predetermined and fantasy-based idea. In just the same way we tend often to assimilate people to their social roles or specific character-istics: we see them as wives or mistresses, as black or Jewish, as upper- or lower-class; thereby acting under the pressure of a categorisation-system that satisfies our own fantasies, fears and desires rather than doing justice to the real world of individual *people.*

In advancing the RF and the BF for the reader's consideration, and in asking him to keep them in mind during Part II of this book (when we consider some specific educational topics), I must again stress that I do not insist on this particular typology of fantasy. Such is the amount of sheer rubbish talked and practised in education, indeed, that one is tempted to identify and name many other fantasies. There is, for instance, the Egalitarian Fantasy, which seems to suppose that making simple-minded sociological moves (destreaming, com-prehensivisation, etc.) will 'break down class barriers' rather than — for human envy is a psychological constant, and human differences an inexpellably logical constant — merely sweep the decks clear so that other (perhaps worse) differences and barriers can replace them. There is the Bureaucratic or Administrative Fantasy, which assimilates educating people to producing motor-cars or collecting taxes, and which thus fails to take into account the structure necessary for any serious education (for instance, that educators rather than administrators hold the power) (cf. J. Wilson, 1977, ch. 2). Many of these, at least, assimilate fairly easily into the RF and the BF: thus the Egalitarian Fantasy is an aspect of the former, the Bureaucratic Fantasy of the latter. But if the reader finds some that do not thus assimilate, I should not be surprised or alarmed: the typology is not intended as exhaustive.

One further admission or explanation: some fantasies are so deep-rooted and so pervasive that it is hard to bring them uniquely under either heading. Take, for instance, the (alarmingly common) general idea that we might want to put at once under the RF heading because it sometimes expresses itself in such phrases as 'Truth is relative', 'There's no such thing as right and wrong, mental health, etc.' But suppose (as is common) the speaker then says 'Truth is what a particular society says is true' ('For people in the Middle Ages the earth *was* flat'), 'Mentally ill is only what a society calls mentally ill', and so on. That now looks like the BF, committing the classic error of identifying a transcendental notion with its particular institution-alisation. The difficulty of classification here, or one of the difficulties, is that such a person swings about, very rapidly, between the RF and the BF: on the one hand, 'There's no such thing as truth'; on the other, 'Truth is what society says it is' — sometimes apparently wishing to excise words from the English language (as if they named something totally non-existent); at other times wishing to give them a different meaning from the usual one.

In introducing the topics covered by the next part of this book, then, I offer the RF and the BF only as the most general guides. I think they will be found useful ones, if only because I myself have found them so. But nothing prevents the reader from conducting his own psychotherapy, so to speak, on the material — indeed I would encourage him to do so. No doubt, too, I sometimes betray fantasies of my own, which should emerge in the lack of clarity, or incompetence or sheer wrong-headedness of what I have to say about these topics. If the reader can detect and identify these for what they are, so much the better. No man should come anywhere near to pretending to freedom from fantasy: such a claim would argue a grotesque fantasy of its own. In this business we can only work together, trying to help ourselves and each other to stay, or become, sane.

PART II

CHAPTER 4

Education and its Requirements

Elsewhere I have tried to make clear at some length the two most common mistakes made when people try to say what education is or is about (J. Wilson, 1979). They are, roughly, (i) the idea that what is marked by 'education' is entirely open or (in the jargon) 'contestable', so that we can pump whatever values and preferences we like into the concept; and (ii) the idea that 'education' can be translated without loss into a particular set of social practices and institutions.

These two mistakes suggest the RF and the BF respectively, as we have already hinted when discussing those fantasies in the last chapter. We need, however, to see in somewhat more detail both (a) the extreme importance of distinguishing education as an enterprise in its own right, different from other enterprises, and also (b) something of the conceptual necessities that go with it.

In order to see something of the ways in which fantasy and incoherence are at work here, perhaps this may best be done by taking *one* illustration of both (a) and (b).

Education and politics

I shall start by a consideration of the relationship between education and politics — a topic commonly discussed by laymen as well as 'experts'. Indeed I shall argue, if only by implication, that the common-sense feeling roughly expressed as 'Education ought to be kept out of politics' is at root entirely sound. Contrast this with the behaviour of some members of the editorial board of one of the most respectable and prestigious educational journals, men both extremely eminent in their profession and hardly to be accused of lack of intelligence or scholarship. In inviting contributions on the topic, they asked contributors to answer the question 'Given that education cannot be taken out of politics, what *should* be the relation between education and politics?' Apart from a lack of clarity (does 'given that' have the force of 'if' or 'since'?), the question seems to imply an identification of 'education' with 'the educational system' (perhaps specifically in certain countries). But that is like saying that morality is to be identified with the moral code of a particular society or societies; or that a 'successful' person is one who is commonly called 'successful' by worldly standards (rich, powerful, etc.). That sort of mistake (arising from the BF) is easy to make, obvious when pointed out, and extremely dangerous.

Let us see what happens if we avoid this mistake and try another tack. There is some difficulty in knowing what could be *meant* by saying that education should (not) or could (not) be 'kept out of' politics. Rather than attempt to resolve this by a direct confrontation of the question 'What are we to demarcate by the terms "education" and "politics"?', it may be better to begin with some parallels. Consider such human activities or enterprises as chess, religion, science, music and medicine. Then there would, I think, be a good deal of common ground, including the following:

(1) Since these activities, at least characteristically and perhaps necessarily, are pursued in a society, they are always able to be affected by social considerations. Some of these we might want to call 'political', including perhaps (a) the 'high' politics of government, party pressures, edicts from sovereign bodies, etc.; (b) the less formal pressures from various groups (students, nurses, Women's Lib.); (c) the tactical considerations that arise in committees and other such situations (often called 'political'). Others such as a shortage of money we might prefer to call 'economic'; others again, such as the pressures of fashion or ideals, it would be hard to classify under a single heading. Thus what actually happens in the world of chess is always liable to be influenced by (i) 'political' ('diplomatic'?) considerations, for instance in relationships with the USSR; (ii) economic considerations — how much money is available for coaching young players, holding attractive tournaments, etc.; and (iii) a rag-bag of 'social' considerations, such as the increased popularity of the game after Fisher's victory in the world title matches.

(2) Nor, again, could it be easily claimed that certain features of life could be permanently identified as 'politically' important and other features be similarly disqualified (and thus seen as immune from such considerations). Wearing green is a political issue in modern Ireland, as it was in ancient Byzantium. There is no such safe ground, because political passions may, with or without reason, attach themselves to any feature of the world. Egalitarians might object to chess because its symbols represent a monarchical system; the Chinese may object to Beethoven because he was a 'bourgeois' composer; and notoriously the practice of science and psychotherapy may be forced to yield to totalitarian pressures.

(3) Nor could any sensible person deny that it would sometimes, at least, be *right* for these activities to be thus affected. For these considerations, more or less *ex hypothesi*, include at least some that such a person would be bound to regard as of overriding importance; or, anyway, of *more* importance than that the activities should be left totally and permanently undisturbed. We should be prepared at least to modify, if not abandon, our practice of chess, music, etc. under the threat of starvation, nuclear war, the persecution and torture of minority groups, and no doubt plenty of other things besides. Even the most fanatical religious believer (to take the most awkward case) would, I think, give some ground here. He might try to protect his practice more fiercely than the scientist, doctor, musician, chess-player, etc.; but it is hard to think of a sane person who would give up *no* element, however small, of the whole apparatus of ritual, symbolism, verbal formulation and so on that he would prefer (if politically or socially undisturbed) to retain, if the alternative were (say) a global holocaust or the prolonged torture of millions of people. At the very least, he might himself refuse to give any such ground (and take the consequences), but would be unlikely to recommend such behaviour to all other people.

All this is just a rather laborious way of saying (i) that, since all activities go on in a society (*polis*), they are necessarily affected by what is believed or done in that society ('politics'); (ii) that these beliefs, actions and happenings may be of almost any kind; and (iii) that in some cases, at least, this is perfectly right and proper. But, as I have suggested, nobody in his senses wants to deny all this. What is it, then, that a person might wish to add to such truisms, if he wanted to make some important point to differentiate these activities from 'politics'?

He might want to make some fairly obvious logical or conceptual points:

(1) First, there is plainly something different in my deciding to make a certain move in chess (a) because it is a losing move and I wish to placate my rich uncle against whom I am playing, or because it is a move recommended by Chairman Mao, or because it involves less expenditure of energy than other moves; and (b) because the position over the board suggests to me that this move is the best one. The difference is that there is an activity, (enterprise, *techne*, rule-governed system), which we demarcate by 'chess', that in a fairly obvious sense incorporates its own standards, principles, and (if one must use the word) 'values'. Like science, music, medicine and — as Aristotle says — all other human activities, it 'aims at some good'. Hence there will be a crucial difference in the *kinds of reasons* a man may use when conducting such an activity in practice: either he will use reasons that are extraneous to the activity, as in (a) above, or reasons that are internal to it, as in (b). A natural way of describing the situation when a man uses (a)-type reasons is to say that he is, to that extent and at that time, not really concerned with *this* activity at all. Objections to Beethoven because he was 'bourgeois' are not *musical* objections, in the way that an objection (say) that he used the trombones too much would be; just as, if I make a losing move because I am trying to placate my opponent, what I am interested in is not *chess* but something else — money, or personal relationships, or whatever. The primary school child who, given $3+3$, makes an 8 out of it by turning the second 3 upside down and joining it to the first would be acting not as a mathematician but, perhaps, as a primitive artist.

(2) Second, another point of logic: if these activities are to be conducted at all in practice, then there must be *some* scope for the operation of the reasons proper to them — what I have called internal ((b)-type) reasons. For there to be, in practice, such things as science, art, chess, etc. there must be people able and willing to believe and act on such reasons. If everything that I do is dictated by political (or social, or any other extraneous) considerations, then I cannot engage in such activities; for the practice of the

activities is defined by my being able to grasp and use the reasons proper to it: the reasons, one might say, that *constitute* it. If every detail of the treatment I hand out to, say, sick people in a concentration camp is dictated by political considerations, then I am not engaging in anything that can seriously be called 'medicine' or 'curing people'. It may overlap with or masquerade as medicine; I may be paid by the Ministry of Health; books may be written about it and classified under 'medicine' in libraries. But it is not medicine: just as, if I move pieces on a chess-board simply so that they appear in aesthetically pleasing positions, and without any regard for the rules and principles of the game, I am not playing chess — except, at best, *per accidens.*

(3) Third, yet another conceptual point: if these activities really do pursue a genuine good (as medicine pursues health, for instance), then there will be at least a *prima facie* case for so arranging society (or 'politics') that the activities can be pursued. Most of the practical arguments here will be about priorities: that is, about the comparative importance of various goods. Some, perhaps less important or peculiarly difficult to arrange for, may have to disappear altogether in certain contexts: for instance, in time of war, plague or famine. But in general it will, necessarily, be right to *try* to cater for the activities; which means acknowledging the existence of the various goods and — a point of great practical importance — understanding just what they are. I stress this last necessity, because it seems to me both surprising and alarming that 'education' is not commonly accepted as a verbal marker for an activity (or group of activities) of this kind. It is, surely, entirely clear that there is an enterprise, roughly to be described as 'the promotion of the serious learning of human beings as such', that must (for a variety of reasons) be regarded as a desirable enterprise, and for which 'education' is a natural marker in our language. Exactly what content we should give to this description (what should count as 'serious', what knowledge is really important, etc.) is of course to be argued about, just as we can (and do) argue about the content to be assigned to general descriptions of science, art, psychotherapy and most other activities. But if someone were to say that there could be no such enterprise, or that *anything* could satisfy such a description, or that the enterprise was in principle an undesirable one, or that 'education' was not a

reasonable marker for it, we should find it hard to understand him.

There will, as with other activities, be a class of reasons — 'educational' reasons — to be contrasted with other kinds of reasons, including 'political' ones. For instance, a certain kind of school organisation might be desirable (a) because it pacified certain political parties, or increased the national wealth, or made the children better able to get good jobs; or (b) because it enabled teachers to teach better and children to learn more. The natural thing to say here is that (a) incorporates non-educational reasons, perhaps to be described as 'political' or 'economic' or 'social', and that (b) points to educational reasons. Of course they may overlap. My purpose here is not to draw an exact distinction between the two, but more simply to point out that if 'education' is allowed to demarcate an activity that pursues a certain kind of good, then it follows that there must be reasons internal to it that can be distinguished from other kinds of reasons. In practice we know this quite well, particularly in negative cases: in war-time or other critical situations we think it right to do all sorts of things with and for children, but would never want to say that these things were all good for their *education*. So too we are prepared to say that a person's education should sometimes give way to other considerations — his duty to look after his aged parents or to fight for his country, or whatever. It is one thing to argue about where these distinctions — which we do in fact make — are to be drawn; quite another to talk as if there was no distinction to be made. Not everything counts as education; not every reason is an educational reason; not every good is an educational good. We may hold differing opinions on how far, in particular social contexts or historical periods, political or other reasons should prevail over educational ones; what we cannot intelligibly do is to talk as if there were nothing to argue about.

If we were to stick fairly closely to some of the points just made, rather as Plato seems sometimes to do (e.g. in Books 1 and 2 of the *Republic*), we might want to deny that education *could* ever be 'in' (or 'taken out of') politics. For on this basis 'education' would name a time-free and culture-free enterprise or *techne* with its own set of reasons; as soon as we stop using these reasons, we stop doing education. Whether we ought to take this Platonic line might depend on what actual problems we want to confront; but it is worth noticing that we do, in practice, often take it — and not without point. Thus if a man's actions or beliefs, which might initially be thought to be governed by the enterprises of science, art or religion, turned out to be governed by politics — if what he did and said about genetics, or abstract painting or the Roman Catholic creed was done and said because he wished to improve or defer to some political situation, rather than because he thought it right or true in terms of the three enterprises — then we should think that he was no longer to be trusted as a scientist, artist or man of religion. Similarly we might want to say that, if a teacher or researcher or administrator did or recommended, in his professional capacity, things that were not supposed to encourage serious learning in pupils, but served quite different ends, we should not trust him as an educator.

There might still be room for 'the relationship between education and politics'. By this we should mean, presumably, that 'society', or 'the government', or whoever, should allow and encourage this enterprise to be practised, insofar as this is thought to be consonant with other goods. That would be virtually the beginning and end of the 'relationship'; for, of course, the people in control of the decisions about *how* it should, in face of competition from other goods, be practised — would have, logically, to be the educators themselves. This would be true by definition; 'educators' would identify that class of people whom we thought best able and willing to understand the particular goods that education aimed at, and to work out how in fact they would be best achieved. (Who these people actually *are*, of course, is a further question: but a question to be answered within the circumscription of education already outlined). On this view, other enterprises (politics, economics, building, etc.) could only relate to education by way of facilitating, supporting, providing supplies or preconditions, and so on — just as government or industry may supply chess-boards, arrange tournaments with prizes, etc. but still have to be distinguished from chess-playing.

Suppose, however, that we do not take this line. Then we are forced into some other account of what 'education' is going to mark. There are at least two obvious candidates here: (i) 'upbringing', i.e. more or less anything we do with children; (ii) the 'educational system', in the sense of those *institutions* that are deemed (whether rightly or wrongly is another question) to be primarily concerned with education in our previous sense — that is, schools, universities and so on. Neither, I think, is a very strong candidate, since clearly

(a) we do *not* describe anything we do to children as 'educating' them — what we so describe is much more strictly delimited; and (b) we could not identify such institutions except by reference to a prior concept of education. But suppose we let these and other objections pass. How then could we approach this 'relationship'?

Candidate (i) would demolish it by expanding it indefinitely. If we raise the question 'What should we do with our children?', then all sorts of answers, relevant in all sorts of contexts, and using all sorts of reasons, immediately become possible. Children may have to be cuddled, cured, given pocket-money, made to dig for victory, or even sacrificed on occasion to preserve the state. The art of distinguishing and adjudicating between these goods, or of framing some ideal situation in which as many as possible would be satisfied, might (in a Greek sense) be termed 'politics'; educational and political theory would then be more coextensive, as in the *Republic.*

Candidate (ii) is equally intractable, since almost everything depends on the particular context. We at once want to know what institutions, in what societies, at what times, under what pressures, with what resources, and so forth. In some situations we think that enterprises like education should be more decentralised and its institutions more autonomous; in others, the reverse. So too (as we saw earlier) with any other enterprise: insofar as certain elements in the practice, or perhaps the entire practice, of science, or art or religion do genuinely wreck or corrupt the state, then they have to be suppressed. We might think poorly of any state of which this was true; but that is simply to repeat the point that a properly organised state will find room for the pursuit of these goods.

One might believe that some generalisations can be made at least about the prevailing temptations that might pull us one way or the other. Yet even this seems doubtful. Athens-loving liberals will point to the ultimately self-defeating totalitarianism of ancient Sparta; but their opponents can point out the weakness inherent in even the most deliciously liberal society if it cannot win wars or cure plagues. Similar arguments might be repeated in terms of the power-blocks today. The argument is complicated by the circularity of the obvious facts (a) that *some* degree of education, some serious learning, is required for survival and a minimum of material prosperity, in any society; (b) that survival and prosperity are required for the practice of education.

It may be thought that these somewhat bleak conceptual points, issuing as they do in largely negative conclusions, are not of much use. That would not be my own judgement. Most of the practical mistakes we make, I believe, are made because of the almost universal confusion between different types of goods and enterprises. We can get nowhere if we do not make these distinctions and plan our practices on the basis of them. If, for instance, governments were to make very specific demands of schools in terms of political goods — that pupils should be turned out economically viable, reasonably law-abiding, literate, etc. — and made it quite clear to the educators that, beyond the range of these demands, it was the educators' job to determine what pupils should learn and how, we should at least have some kind of structure for our arguments.

Examinations

Out of the many conceptual necessities that education brings with it (described in more detail in J. Wilson, 1977, 1979), I single out the notion marked by 'examination' — partly because it is a fairly simple and obvious case, and partly because some of the relevant ground has not (so far as my reading goes) been covered. Indeed, in view of the constancy and intensity of disputes that are conducted under this heading, it is a little shocking that the topic has not (so far as I am aware) been treated with much intellectual seriousness. There is, of course, plenty of passion and fashion — nowadays, mostly tending to favour cutting down or abolishing 'exams' — and plenty of desperate quasi-bureaucratic attempts, by such bodies as the Schools Council, to invent new types of examinations at different 'levels' that will make 'the system' more flexible or in other ways acceptable. But there are obviously some prior and important questions to be asked here. At least we must try to get clear (i) what we are talking about under the title of 'examinations', and (ii) what examinations are for.

These questions are plainly connected; but it is important to start with (i), because of a point of methodology that has devastated discussion in this particular area, and that has implications for other areas also. Just as (for instance), when the words 'religion' or 'morality' are mentioned, many people think only of the particular religion or moral code with which they are most familiar, so when there is talk of 'examinations' it is often taken for granted that some particular examinations or system of examining must be meant — in the UK, perhaps, the system of 'O' and 'A' levels, or 'CSE', or the idea of written examinations at the end of a college course, or whatever it may be. Then, if one disapproves of this particular system, one may find oneself in favour of 'abolishing examinations'; and this may easily (by a sort of forgetfulness) come to mean *all* examinations, even though what was disapproved of was originally one particular system. In much the same way people may slide, as it were, from talking of particular religious faiths or moral codes into talking of religion and morality in general, and carry their attitudes with them as they slide. We have to step firmly back from all this, and consider in a more general way what sorts of things we are discussing here.

A simple loosening move is to remember some of the terms that might be coextensive, or partly overlap, with 'examine': 'test', 'assess', 'evaluate', 'investigate', 'check up', 'review' and so on. The root idea is just that of trying to *find out* something by a fairly close *scrutiny*. One may examine a patient suspected of a disease, or examine a firm's accounts, or even examine the back of one's hand for spots. A person can do this out of idle curiosity (I may not mind one way or another whether I have spots on the back of my hand); but, since human beings usually act purposively, with certain goods or objectives in mind, the point of examining things is nearly always related to these goods or their opposites. We want to know how the patient is progressing, whether the firm's accounts are properly kept, and so on.

These (extremely obvious) points remind us that a world in which we did not examine things for various purposes would be inconceivable. So long as we prefer some states of affairs to others and so long as we have minds — and these two features are themselves part of what is meant by being human or rational — we shall inevitably make some attempt to discover by scrutiny how things are in relation to our goods. It would be difficult or impossible to know what could be *meant* by anyone who said that we ought not to examine things or people, in this (normal) sense of 'examine'. He might perhaps mean that we should not spend too much time examining them, and we could argue about how much is 'too much'; more probably he has lapsed into tying 'examine' down to some particular form of examination to which he — perhaps justly — objects.

This might not need saying, were it not that we feel ambivalently about the whole process. A part of us very much wants to know, by 'examining', how things stand both as regards our own selves (interests, abilities, performances, etc.) and as regards those of other people; but another part very much dislikes the idea of knowing. When the latter part is dominant — as it often is in some individuals or climates of opinion — we may talk as if the whole idea of putting 'labels' on people or 'categorising' them were somehow wrong; even though we know, in our saner moments, that we could not think or talk at all without the use of labels and categories. We may feel that the whole business of grading, passing and failing, and assessing people (particularly the young) as such-and-such is in a way distasteful, or perhaps unjust, or anyhow imperfect. And this may tempt us to speak out against the entire enterprise. It is a very general feeling ('abolishing examinations' is just one aspect of it), and has much to do with notions of 'integrating' and 'segregating' people in general. We see here the clear operation of the RF; the idea that there are, ultimately, no 'valid standards' allows us to dispense with the whole enterprise.

Of course there are some important points to be made here: perhaps particularly the point that there are *other* things to be done with people besides grade them — for instance, teach them, encourage them, help them and so on; and that there are some human relationships, perhaps of particular significance, within which the notion of grading could not always coherently apply — to love somebody has more to do with identifying and 'belonging' to the person than with seeing him as satisfying some impersonal criteria of goodness. We may fear that grading may, by proliferation or undue emphasis, close the doors on these other things. There are many deep psychological difficulties here that need investigation. But it remains clear that, despite some very real dangers, any idea that we could do without the general notion and practice of 'examining' or grading would be a kind of fantasy. The notion is inexpellable.

Such considerations may perhaps help us to look, with a less parochial eye, at some very general questions that naturally arise. *Prima facie* these might be put into two groups. First, what sort of things do we want to examine or assess? Who should do the assessing, and how should it be done? Second, for whose benefit or for what purposes are these assessments? In practice, as we shall see, however, the connections between the two groups of questions are too close to make any neat divisions. I shall begin, somewhat arbitrarily, with some points about who *needs* examinations; remembering always that we are discussing not any given 'function' or 'social function' of an existing examination system but the (apparently) simpler question of who needs the information that examinations logically must provide — that is, assuming that they are in any degree successful.

If we are considering examinations, still in this broad sense, for schools or pupils, the most natural (though for some perhaps the most surprising) answer to the question 'Who needs examinations?' seems to be 'The pupils themselves'. If I am in the position of a learner, whether by choice or compulsion, clearly I will have an interest in knowing how much I have learned or how much progress I have made. To be concerned with anything conceptually implies concern with checking up on that thing as and when necessary: with verifying whether it is in the sort of state I want it to be in. I check to see whether my bank balance, house, motor-bike, cat, etc. are all right. Of course I can be neurotic or obsessional about this; but there is a straight contradiction implied in saying that I care about X but do not care to find out whether X is as it should be. If someone said that he was interested in (say) learning to read or do sums but did not wish to know what progress he was making, we should not understand him.

This rather bleak conceptual point may not seem to cover much ground — though it may help us distinguish people who say they are, or are thought to be, seriously interested in X from those who are actually so interested. A person who really wants to have something at his fingertips will naturally welcome — for his own benefit — all kinds of checks, tests, examinations and other ways of verifying. He wants to be *sure* that he knows and can rely on his knowledge. In cases where we are serious — where our lives may depend upon it — this is obvious enough: the mountaineer welcomes a close examination of his rope, the deep-sea sailor of his hull, the soldier of his rifle. The point reinforces the central importance, to education in general, of getting pupils to be serious about learning anything (cf. J. Wilson, 1979).

But (it will be said) this point alone does not establish the desirability of any kind of public or 'competitive' examination. Could not the teacher, or perhaps even the pupil himself, assess his progress — why must it be public? And could his progress not be judged purely individually, rather than compared with that of other pupils — why must it be 'competitive'? There are some conceptual points, if of a rather looser kind, that show the weakness of these suggestions. First, almost anything that a pupil can seriously learn will be necessarily subject to public standards. Any description of a state of having learned something — 'being able to read', 'appreciating Shakespeare', 'competent at mathematics', 'a good guitar-player' — is inevitably a public description, to be publicly verified. The public standards of verification may, of course, be incorporated in other forms than what we call 'public examinations': in the mind of a teacher, in books, in self-administered tests and so on. The most natural and fool-proof method of assessment, however, looks as if it might be a standard examination that properly encapsulates whatever we mean by 'able to read' ('appreciate Shakespeare', etc.): something that is not subject to the vagaries of meaning that different teachers might give to such phrases, or to the vagaries of practical assessment ('marking') by different people. The best people to conduct such assessments would presumably be those who knew enough about the subject-matter being assessed and were best able to judge progress in it. The latter point is crucial: to be very good at a subject — a university professor, for instance — does not necessarily mean that one is good at judging progress at lower levels.

These considerations also suggest the unreality — I think, the conceptual impossibility — of examinations that are in *no* sense 'competitive': that is, of a pupil's progress being judged purely in relation to itself — a nonsensical phrase that precisely indicates the difficulty. The pupil has to meet public standards; and, unless he is kept in complete isolation, it is hard to see how he can avoid being aware that other people besides himself are also trying to meet them — that is, trying to learn things or do things. It will inevitably become clear to him, however much we try to mask it, that other pupils do better or worse than he does. Indeed, the point may be even stronger. *Could* a child learn to talk, for instance, or learn to behave in many other ways, without having the background idea of talking 'like Mummy and Daddy do'? Are not some of these public standards necessarily incorporated, for the child, in *people* who satisfy them — and, for the most part, satisfy them better than he does? Without pressing this, I think it is clear that the notion of removing personal comparison or competition is a radically unrealistic one.

Again, it does not follow from this that any *particular* systems of public or competitive examination are desirable (or undesirable). If an educational régime is so stringent that doing worse at Latin than other boys makes me permanently depressed or suicidal, or that doing better gives me delusions of grandeur — well, there is something wrong; though it has to be remembered that it is not necessarily the *system* that is wrong — maybe I am an insecure child and would feel like this whatever criteria of success and failure are used (as some, inevitably, must be). The answer may not lie in changing the criteria, but in doing whatever can be done to improve my self-confidence. But it does follow, surely, that what many practising teachers describe as the 'natural' tendency of children to want to measure their strength, abilities, attainments and so on against other children (and adults) is perfectly right and proper — to some extent, perhaps logically inevitable. The word 'against' need not imply hostility; nor need we be frightened by 'competitive'. Many activities (particularly games) would be impossible without 'competition', but there is no reason to believe that this in itself generates hostility or any other undesirable state of affairs. One could perfectly well describe, say, a chess-game or cricket match as something like a work of art that the players cooperated to construct in the friendliest of ways, and, conversely, a supposedly 'cooperative' enterprise — say, building a school hut — in which pupils in fact 'competed' furiously with each other and in which there was no fellow-feeling or friendship at all.

I am claiming, then, that the pupils themselves need some examinations of this kind — that is, of a public kind — whereby they can measure themselves objectively against the public standards of whatever they are learning (and, inevitably, against the performances of other people in the same business). I incline to think — though this is a psychological question — that this is a point of extreme importance for the pupil's security, in two general ways. First, the pupil wants to know where he is in relation to what he is doing; he does not want to feel lost in an unstructured morass. He needs — perhaps particularly when he is young — very clear reference points or signposts that will tell him how he is doing. The whole business, now often condemned as 'old-fashioned', of marks, gold stars, clean copy-books and so on appears in this light as something that is far from silly: something (I am tempted to say) that anyone who actually *knew* what young children were like could only reject under the influence of the RF. Secondly, there is the connected point that he has to learn to tolerate the experiences of success and failure that the application of public criteria — 'examinations' — give him. He has to learn that the world does not come to an end if he gets bad marks, and that heaven's gates do not open if he gets good ones; and he has, surely, to learn this in relation to other people's performances when compared with his own. Of course he will not learn this if he is not sufficiently supported by love, help and encouragement; but it is something he must learn all the same, and we do not make it easier for him to learn it by removing the opportunities for learning.

It is also perfectly clear that other classes of people need examinations. Amongst these are (i) those who have an immediate interest in the pupil's progress, namely his teachers and others directly concerned with encouraging that progress (parents, for example); (ii) those who have an interest not, or not only, in the progress itself, but in particular attainments, abilities, attitudes and so on that are required for other tasks: for instance, employers and those who may teach the pupil later in his career (e.g. in higher education). These needs are incorporated in the questions (a) 'Are we succeeding in *our* job with the pupil?', and (b) 'Does the pupil have such-and-such characteristics, which are *required for* such-and-such a job or position?' Again, there is a conceptual inevitability about the need to ask and answer such questions. If employers, selectors in higher education and so on did not ask them, and did not seek to get as much relevant information as they could, we should say that they were not really serious about selecting the right people.

An important sub-class of (ii), it may here be noted, consists of the state or the community as a whole. There are certain *a priori* requirements for running any sort of society or community: for instance, that most or at least enough people should be able to pull their economic weight, understand and keep the laws most of the time, perhaps defend the community when necessary, and so on. These requirements in fact cover a good deal of ground; and though many of them may be delegated to parents and teachers, if a government or state authority was not in some degree concerned to check up on whether pupils were in fact able to meet the requirements, we should again have to say that such a government was not seriously concerned with keeping the society going. This remains true, whatever the outcome of various arguments about what sort of society we want, simply because some *a priori* requirements exist for any society.

So far I have done no more than sketch certain fairly obvious conceptual requirements that seem undeniable. The general effect of this, I hope, is to show that 'the system' of examinations that we and most other societies have does at least represent *some* practical attempt to meet these requirements — though, perhaps, a very incompetent one. Instead of asking 'Should we have examinations, assessment-procedures for the benefit of pupils, employers, teachers, the state, etc., or shouldn't we?' it now seems more reasonable to ask 'Given that we can see, in general terms, the necessity for these, how can we improve on the particular forms?' And to say this is not necessarily to commit oneself to some 'empiricist' or 'piecemeal' theory of social change; it may well be that very dramatic changes are required — only, they will be changes of *format*: the conceptual requirements are unchangeable.

Clearly it is a herculean task to give any thorough and detailed answer to such questions, and one that could in principle only be successfully achieved by a long-term research project conducted under appropriate conditions (described in J. Wilson, 1972a). As so often in education, much of this would be a matter of first creating an adequate taxonomy or set of categorisations, later to be backed up by empirical facts and experimentation. Our two general questions — what should we examine, and for whose benefit? — need to be broken down into much more detail. We should need, at least, to ask (i) what needs to be examined, (ii) by what methods, (iii) who arranges and evaluates the examination, (iv) who is examined, (v) how often and under what conditions they are examined, (vi) for whose benefit the information is thus gained, (vii) what sort of benefits gaining this information may bring, (viii) what actual or possible side-effects the process has. Even this list no doubt needs additions; but if individual teachers and others at least ask the questions, it may be that common sense and a bit of imagination will take us a long way.

Much of what we do will turn on getting clear about individual cases in (i) — *what* is to be examined. A good deal of the current dislike of examinations is perhaps engendered by the (true or false) idea that they demand only 'factual knowledge', 'rote learning' or 'a good memory', and favour 'the good examinees' rather than pupils with more imagination, 'creativity' or other qualities. If so, we have to set about the task of determining how to examine or assess these other things. This involves deciding how much we are concerned with (a) purely 'factual knowledge', (b) conceptual competence and ability in a particular discipline, (c) imagination within it, and so on; and/or — thinking now not of a particular subject or discipline but of the pupil's performances more generally — (d) his 'creativity', (e) 'motivation', (f) determination, (g) seriousness and so on in life as a whole.

All this is no doubt very alarming, and may cause some people to regress to the notion that some things, including some of the most important, 'can't be examined'. This has to be resisted, and we have to remember the conceptual point that anything describable must be, at least in principle, able to be verified. If we really *mean* anything by 'determined', 'imaginative', 'kind', 'bad at concentrating', and so on, then there must be *something* observable about the pupil that enables us to predicate such terms of him. Of course the correct form of assessment may not be a written question-paper; but there must, logically, be ways of finding out.

It is a striking phenomenon, I think, that those who most often complain about written examinations on the grounds that they do not get at what is really 'important' about pupils — perhaps their good-heartedness, or seriousness, or imagination, or whatever — also seem those who most dislike the idea of examining in any form at all. The moral or personal development of pupils, for instance, is commonly assessed (in private boarding schools and elsewhere) by the pupils' housemaster or headmaster, who may write quite a long termly report on each pupil as a result of his observations. But this is not commonly done, or even seriously attempted, in other schools that make great play with notions like 'concern', 'caring', 'creative cooperation' and so forth. Naturally one would hope for better or more precise methods of examination than we now have; my point is that such things can be assessed in principle, and that what prevents them being assessed in practice is as much lack of will as lack of technique.

It is fairly easy to see how the BF is likely to intervene at this point. The BF reaction would be something like 'Yes, yes, of course we must examine: we can't let teachers just charge ahead without evaluating their success as teachers — think of all the public money involved, let alone parental concern. So we must demand of them a very detailed, careful and scientifically assessable set of objectives'. This is the 'behavioural objectives' approach, about which we need say little: for, as often, it turns out either to do no more than make very obvious (indeed conceptually necessary) points or — more usually — to display all the marks of an extremist BF.

Nobody denies that, if someone learns something, there must be

— at least in principle, however hard it may be to get at it — some kind of change in that person. It may emerge in his overt (physical) behaviour; in his conversation; in the answers he can give to various questions; in his general attitude; or in his inner thoughts. But if he has learned it, there must be a difference in him; otherwise it would make no sense to say that he had learned it. (If something has happened, then something has happened). But also, no sane person denies that the difference need not involve behaviour — unless 'behaviour' is stretched to cover *any* kind of change. The person who appreciates Beethoven or Shakespeare, or who grasps a philosophical truth, may *behave* no differently: we do not think that we can verify what has happened by taking photographs, or measuring his eye pupils, or watching him *do* things (in any usual sense of 'do'). What has changed are his *feelings* and *understanding.* That change will of course emerge in some form or other — perhaps in the general good sense or insight displayed when he writes an essay, perhaps in conversation with those who are farther along the road of understanding than he is.

Quite obviously, any evaluation or assessment or examination of what X has learned will depend (as we have said) almost entirely on the nature of what he has learned. We do not, and could not intelligibly, examine philosophical understanding, literary appreciation, mathematical competence and so on in the same way. Some items of learning (the 'hard facts') will lend themselves to one form of evaluation, others (a deeper understanding, or competence in the subject generally) to other forms. Someone who attempted to evaluate philosophical competence by a multiple-choice question ('Is the will free? Yes/no'; 'Are ethics (a) objective, (b) subjective, (c) somewhere in between? Put a tick in the relevant box') would not know what philosophical competence was.

There is then (as usual) no way forward except by hard work. We have to consider just *what it means* to be good at French, competent at mathematics, or whatever our objectives may be; and from clarity about these will follow, fairly quickly and obviously in most cases, the forms of examination we need. So long as we keep clear of the RF, which tempts us to suppose that there is no such thing as 'competence' or 'correctness' or 'standards' in (say) creative writing, religious belief or political opinion, and of the BF, which tempts us to assimilate all understanding to the natural sciences, progress is possible.

CHAPTER 5

Educational Research

I turn next to educational research, an area in which both the RF and the BF are very obvious. Many people, I think, have grave doubts about the merits and usefulness of educational research; but their criticisms usually miss the mark because they do not uncover the basic difficulties. Thus it is often said, by those outside the business (particularly teachers), that it is 'not practical' or 'not useful', with the implication that if only researchers were more 'in touch with the classroom' things would be much better; and those in the business often criticise particular pieces of research on grounds of technique (the kind of 'sample' the researcher takes, the reliability of the tests he uses, and so on), with the implication that if we were only rather more careful about our 'research methods' everything would be all right. These criticisms are not without force; but both assume that what now goes on under the heading of 'educational research' is basically sound and sensible. That is, in my judgement, quite untrue. It is not intellectually respectable but fantasy-dominated (that is *why* it is of little practical use), and what is wrong is a matter not so much of carelessly used but reputable techniques or 'research methods', but of certain myths or gross misconceptions that pervade the whole enterprise. I shall try to spell these out now.

'Values'

The first myth is that educational research should be (so far as possible) 'value-free'. It results, as we shall see, either from the RF (that there are no 'objective' values anyway), or from the BF (that what is valuable is a matter of sociological fact — for instance, that it is what governments want or what a 'general consensus' incorporates).

Research in technology or the natural sciences can often, without impropriety, be pursued whilst taking two sorts of things as 'given': first, the desirability of the end product; and second, certain more or less fixed practical possibilities and impossibilities relevant to achieving it. Thus if called upon to consider sending a rocket to the moon, for instance, the researcher may often legitimately (i) avoid consideration of whether rockets *ought* to be sent to the moon, and (ii) work within at least some given parameters, such as whether the society sponsoring the work could conceivably afford such an enterprise, or whether current technology is anywhere near sophisticated enough.

One of the disasters of most educational research (due ultimately to the BF) has been to make more or less similar assumptions: briefly, both (i) to take for granted the 'values' imposed on or suggested to researchers by governments, 'society', research sponsors, etc., and (ii) to assume that certain 'facts', often of a social or political nature, should be taken as given in much the same way as we might take lack of money or the law of gravity as given. I shall argue that this not only prevents educational research from being intellectually respectable, but also makes its results disastrous in practice.

The more obvious mistake is the taking of 'values' for granted. 'Sending a rocket to the moon' is a value-free description; 'educating people' (in respect of any subject, topic or mental power) is not — it normally contains the idea of *improvement*, not just a change of attitude or behaviour. Further, it contains the idea of a certain *kind* of improvement: roughly, a gain in understanding, or rationality, or knowledge, or awareness, coming from *learning.* If, by brainwashing or a skilful advertising campaign, we succeeded in persuading people that black was beautiful, we should not thereby have educated them.

It will thus be an essential part of any research in education to consider just what improvements in understanding the research is aimed at, and what sort of empirical knowledge or 'findings' is relevant to these improvements. This presents problems even in school subjects (mathematics, history, etc.), and graver problems still in research that may go on under headings like 'moral education', 'education for social change', 'enabling the child to adjust to society', and so forth. In particular, to take the kind of norms or aims incorporated in research-summaries approved by governments or sponsoring bodies as given, rather than confronting the question of how far these can be seen as *educational* aims, must be a bad mistake: analogous, to take an extreme case, to assuming simply that what the Nazi authorities want us to find out about improving the Hitler Youth Movement or making gas-chambers more efficient could seriously count as educational research. Aims cannot, logically, just be taken over from governments, or teachers, or a 'general consensus', or 'society', or anything else; it is, necessarily, a major task in the research to work out what is educationally valuable — just as medical researchers would be concerned to work out (if there were any confusion about this) what was valuable for *health*. The notion of education brings its own goods or benefits with it; but these often get confused with other types of benefits, or even with objectives that may not involve benefits at all.

More disputable is the question of what 'facts' to take for granted. My complaint here is that we have lost our nerve, or perhaps our common sense, and take too many political facts as immutable: regarding them more like laws of nature, when they may only survive because of the false perceptions or mental confusion of men. Most of us have some sort of intuitive understanding about these parameters. We have to assume that we cannot, in the immediate or foreseeable future, double the number of teachers, or only allow teachers with IQs of over 170, or spend on education ten times as much as we now spend. Conversely, we should not assume that a new method of teaching French, or a new attitude to religious education, was impracticable simply because there might be difficulties in getting teachers to understand or adopt it. Much, of course, depends on the circumstances: the chances of getting Nazis or extreme Communists or any other extreme sectarians to adopt a seriously *educational* attitude to morality or religion may well be minimal. But we make a rough, if optimistic, distinction between the less mutable 'hard' facts of money and time and the more mutable 'social' facts of people's opinions and beliefs. If we did not regard the latter as at least more amenable to change, we could hardly remain in the education business at all.

Where our nerve fails, I think, is in confronting institutional arrangements. Consider the generally accepted view that schools are, by and large, less 'potent' or influential than the home background, local community, peer-group pressures and so on. We tend simply to assume that this somehow must be so, and that our research must be directed towards finding out how these other influences can be improved: how we can get more cooperation from parents, ameliorate home backgrounds, etc. The obvious alternative — that of trying to make schools more 'potent' in themselves, by giving teachers more power and scope, perhaps by shielding them from 'society' and enlarging the range and type of influence they may have — is not widely investigated. It is as if we thought that Arnold's Rugby, or anything like a 'total' or properly 'potent' institution, was simply not viable. Yet the arguments for at least considering this are clear enough (and ought to strike us forcibly, in view of the considerable chaos in some schools); it is hard not to believe that 'not viable' here really means only 'not usual' or 'needing a lot of institutional change'.

How acceptable such an alternative would be 'politically' — that is, I suppose, to parents, local communities, governments and so on — turns out to be a very open question — simply because researchers have not, in general, bothered to sketch out the alternative in practicable form and canvass opinion on it. Quite possibly many existing arrangements, however 'usual', are not in fact in accordance with popular opinion at all. In any case, it is the researcher's business to work out what arrangements would best satisfy educational values and present them as such to others. It is certainly not his business to take such supposed 'facts' for granted.

Now let us look more closely at the 'value-free' myth. If the idea was simply that the researcher should not incorporate *his own* particular values, preferences, prejudices or what you will into research, this would not be a myth. Nor, I suppose, is it strictly speaking myth if researchers simply accepted the 'values' from politicians, teachers, fashion or some other source: I should be inclined to call this more of a disgrace ('The Führer knows that it's valuable for all kids to grow up hating Jews: just get to work and tell us how to do this'). The myth is that one can do serious research without oneself tackling the question, just by restricting oneself to 'the facts'.

Consider research into reading. We want 'good readers' or 'competent readers'. But what is to count as a 'good reader'? If you like grand language, this is a 'question of value'; and now, the myth goes, either we must duck this question or else we shall only be using our own 'value-judgements'. Nonsense: what we have to do is to tackle the question; to look at the possible concepts involved. For instance, are we interested only in producing or finding out who can read or (also) who actually does read? Are we to mean by 'a good reader' someone who only reads when under extreme pressure to do so? Again, are we interested only in correct phonetic interpretation of written signs (only the signs used in the English language?), or also in whether he understands what he reads? If the latter, how much understanding? Understanding of what sort of subject-matter? All these questions arise, and more. To try and do 'research into reading' without considering them properly is just crazy — we would not know what research we were doing.

The point is that it is not entirely arbitrary ('a value-judgement') how these questions are answered. We do, in a semi-conscious way, have some idea of what we want to mean by 'a good reader', 'a morally educated person', 'being able to think like a competent scientist', 'breaking down class barriers', 'a sense of failure' and so forth. But this needs to be made conscious and precise, by comparing possible concepts and interpretations. Having done this, it will usually be obvious what we are after; but even if there are possible choices to be made, at least we shall be clear what these are. We can say, for example, 'If by "morally educated" you mean PQR, then we'll do one type of research; if you mean XYZ, we'll do quite another type'.

Getting the 'values' clear and precisely expressed is not only a preliminary to making 'value-judgements' — though it is at least that. Rather, it is the proper way of determining what our values and desires actually are. I do not deny that there can be differences of opinion; but we do not have either to make some arbitrary choice or to accept some arbitrary ruling. In research it is usually not so much a matter of deciding whether we want pupils to be 'mature', 'responsible', 'well educated', and so on; it is a matter of getting clear about what we mean by these terms. Nobody, for instance, wants children to be stupid; but when we come to consider what is meant by 'intelligent' we have a difficult task yet, obviously, an essential one if we are to assess or promote 'intelligence' in any normal sense.

We can see, then, that most educational research — indeed, one is tempted to say, any research that could fairly be described as *educational* — must be 'normative', in the straightforward sense that it must be about whether certain educational objectives are being or should be realised in practice: whether this or that way of teaching English makes pupils better at English, whether mixed or unmixed ability groupings promote academic learning or help to 'break down social barriers', whether pupils flourish better in sixth forms or sixth-form colleges, whether primary school children learn more in an open-plan or a more old-fashioned system, and so on. In other words, unless there is some idea of what counts as *success* in the researched area, it is hard to see how the researcher can even start. This is perhaps most obvious in the case of subject-learning: unless we had some idea, for instance, of what it is to do mathematics *well*, or to know *more* mathematics, or to make *progress* in mathematics, the researcher would have no starting-point from which to make relevant observations — for there would be nothing 'educational' for the observations to be relevant *to*. Nor, of course, would there be any point in doing the research; for to observe people doing different things (using different teaching methods) would be pointless unless we wished to distinguish some methods as more likely to make for progress in mathematics.

It is also clear that a large and crucially important part of the research is precisely to clarify these objectives: that is, both to ensure that they are reasonable in themselves and to put them into an unambiguous form. For example, we might start with the vague idea that 'mixed-ability grouping' tends to 'break down class barriers'; and we should need (i) to be reasonably convinced, after plenty of argument, that this represented a reasonable objective, which would in itself involve (ii) determining what 'mixed-ability grouping' meant, and what was meant by 'class barriers'. Are we, for instance, talking about *ability* or *attainment*? *How* mixed must 'mixed-ability' groups be? What sort of 'class barriers' — just those of social class, or any kind of categorisation of human beings? Until we have answered such questions to our satisfaction, we shall not even know what our research is *about*.

Rather than face these facts, most researchers adopt an attitude that resembles servility rather than modesty. Modesty might lead them to acknowledge that the questions, though well within the range of any reasonably intelligent person who was serious about the need for answering them, might also need the assistance of experts — or at least some careful reading of those (comparatively few) writers in this particular field. Servility backed by the RF and BF in fact leads them to place the responsibility for answering them on other shoulders. The assumption is made, overtly or tacitly, that someone else — teachers, the pupils themselves, a current 'consensus', the politicians or other power-holders who may sponsor or initiate a particular piece of research, or others — has faced these questions and answered them; so that the researcher need only carry on and find out the facts.

The first point about this assumption is that these other people have demonstrably *not* answered the questions satisfactorily, or (for the most part) even faced them. Different creeds, articles of faith and educational climates of opinion do indeed prevail in such quarters; but even — what is certainly not true — if any of these were already known to be true or right (perhaps by some clairvoyant procedure), they would still be of no use to the researcher, simply because they are not stated with sufficient clarity. For instance, even if 'breaking down class barriers' could already be accepted as a good thing for educators to do, research on the topic would still be difficult or impossible unless and until we know what is to *count as* a 'class barrier' and what is to count as it being 'broken down'. Thus suppose barriers of class in the sense of socio-economic rating diminish, but barriers of class in a wider sense (say, between clever and stupid, or old and young, or men and women, or 'trendy' and its opposite) increase: are we to say that class barriers have been broken down or not? Obviously we cannot know *what* to say until we are much clearer than most prevailing educational tenets have made us.

This initial servility — the refusal to tackle the questions for oneself — leads researchers into one of two attitudes. Neither attitude is usually pursued to an extreme, and we might prefer to talk rather of different ranges or admixtures than of any clear distinction here. But, in principle, the researcher can either (a) pursue the task of determining what some *other* person or body takes the answers to be (the BF), or (b) try to deny the force, or forget about, the questions altogether (the RF). If he opted for (a), for instance, he would spend time trying to determine what (say) *teachers* meant by 'mixed ability' or 'class barriers', and what *they* took to be the point and criteria of success in various classroom arrangements; or he might, if extremely servile, try to get a clear statement from the government or from his funding body about what *they* took 'equality of opportunity' or 'the comprehensive spirit' to be. If he opted for (b), he would find himself reduced to some vague attempt merely to 'describe the problems' or 'make a survey of the options' in his researched area: an attempt doomed to failure, since (for reasons given above) even the task of 'description' is impossible except in reference to certain norms. *What* you describe, what *counts* as a 'problem', is already partly determined by some conceptual framework; just as an 'option' is only an option *for some purpose.*

The former, (a), is a form of direct servility to whatever establishment happens to attract one. This remains true even if it is some kind of counter-establishment: much research, even if not worthy the name, is done under the magnetic spell of those who believe in various kinds of radical innovation, 'liberation', 'a revolutionised society', and so on. The most fashionable servility (at least in theory) is to teachers, indicating a rather desperate attempt to be 'relevant' at all costs, and perhaps also a dislike of appearing 'authoritarian' even if this (unintelligible) term is applied only to giving teachers more clarity and some right answers. One teacher made the relevant points very clearly in conversation:

> We don't want researchers to ask *us* what we should be trying to do and how we should do it: we want them to *tell* us if they can. They haven't been able to so far, but that means they should try harder — they can't make up for it by a lot of chummy working-parties and pseudo-democratic conferences. If someone can prove to me that there's a better way of making my kids stop hitting each other and learn their maths quicker, then I'll start listening.

More cowardly than servile, (b) is useless in a more straightforward sense. At least, if (a) is diligently pursued and if those questioned have some clear idea of what they want, the researcher may end up with better ways of giving it them — though, of course, he must not mind if what they want is prejudicial or wicked. But with (b) the very idea of success or any kind of norm is quietly dropped. Comprehensive schools, mixed-ability grouping, alternatives to the sixth form and other fashionable areas are 'surveyed', and some 'facts' determined; but what the surveys *show*, or which way the facts *point,* is naturally invisible — unless, as often happens, some norms (either from current fashion or from the researchers' own prejudices) are smuggled in by the back door.

It will be said — indeed, it often is said — that practical pressures are too great for such questions to be properly tackled. In a less liberal society this might have some plausibility — if one is actually sacked, for instance, for not following the funding body's objectives faithfully enough, or producing unpopular conclusions. (In fact, a good deal of latitude is allowed to researchers in this area, if only because funding bodies and others in the power-structure are

themselves almost entirely unclear in their statements of objectives).
But otherwise the plea is implausible. Few directors of research
tyrannically impose their own particular interpretations (again,
usually because they have not considered the question fully enough);
indeed, and very regrettably, few such directors even encourage or
insist upon clarification of this kind at all. Certainly they do not
actively prevent it. Rather, the researchers themselves simply do not
attempt it.

Shortage of time is no excuse. If research into X means, as it nearly
always will mean, that we have first to get clear about X — well, that
just *is* the researcher's job. Often it can be done soon enough to leave
time for more directly empirical work; but even if it cannot, the
researchers will at least have laid the necessary foundations for
continued work in the area. If researchers had in fact done this, we
should be saved from the constant life-cycles of research projects
that appear to tackle exactly the same areas over and over again
throughout the decades. A really clear account of the basic distinctions and concepts in 'mixed-ability' and 'class barriers' would
mean solid progress, even if few empirical facts had time to emerge.
Moreover, it might well be that *if* we were clear in this way, the facts
might often be extremely obvious — or, perhaps, such as only
teachers on the job could gather.

It would need a good deal of research to explain exactly why
researchers behave in these ways; but one trouble is that the RF and
BF are now thoroughly *institutionalised*. Certain practices and
methods are familiar, and anything outside those practices and
methods seems threatening or likely to cause some kind of trouble.
Various fashions within the familiar terrain may come and go:
'comparative study', 'statistical findings', 'depth interviews' and other
pieces of methodological bric-à-brac may or may not be worn this
year. But having to step outside the entire shop — particularly if
one's job is, or seems to be, at stake — is, very naturally, alarming.
This is particularly a pity in that the climate of opinion, not only
amongst academics in the field but also amongst practising teachers
and the general public, is certainly changing. No doubt disenchanted
by the aloof behaviourism of educational research in earlier times,
they are also rapidly becoming disenchanted by the constant changes
in educational fashion, by the ephemeral demands for 'relevance' and
by the way in which even the most respectable educational research
organisations seem to take their cues more from the fluctuating

demands of society and politicians than from their own good sense — of which, if only they could believe it, they have plenty.

We congratulate ourselves in this country on preserving the purity and freedom of certain enterprises. Unlike the Russians, we are not prepared to describe the conditioning of political dissidents in prison as 'psychotherapy' or 'psychiatry'; unlike the Nazis, we do not give the title of 'scientific research' to the elaboration of fantasies about Aryan blood; unlike the Chinese, we do not think that Beethoven's music is aesthetically poorer because of Beethoven's bourgeois background. But because we lack any clear idea of what the enterprises marked by 'education' and 'educational research' are supposed to be about, we find ourselves unable or unwilling to prevent them being taken over by irrelevant forces.

Even in these egalitarian days, most sane people will admit (albeit reluctantly) to the existence of expertise and authority in many enterprises. However mistaken and incompetent they may be, there are doctors, scientists, music critics and even psychotherapists who know more about their enterprises than the rest of us. If we did not believe this — if we had no idea who was to count as an authority — we should not know to whom we ought to entrust these enterprises and the research necessary for them. We should then be driven either to abandon them or else to conduct them in accordance with political principles. 'Political', in our society, would mean roughly the pushes and pulls of pressure-groups, fashion, 'climate of opinion' and salesmanship; in more authoritarian societies it would mean, more simply, the party line.

This is, I think, essentially our present position in educational research. That it applies to the practice of education is obvious enough: nobody seriously believes (though many fantasise) that changes are made as a result of intellectual progress in the subject, as they are in medicine or engineering, rather than as a result of political or (in a broad sense) moral changes of climate. That it applies also to research, however, is less obvious, if also more alarming. Those familiar with the politics of educational research know well enough how the fashions change; how important it is to keep on the right side of the teachers' unions; how any research must be made to look 'practical', 'relevant', 'democratic', or whatever the current climate may be; and how great the furore would be if it was boldly suggested that there were, or could be, overall authorities who should tell politicians and pressure-groups what to do rather than *vice versa.*

But many ordinary people may still believe that there are acknowledged experts. The fact is that there are not. There are more or less fashionable, and hence powerful, individuals; more commonly, there are more or less variable climates of opinion that distil themselves in the relevant committees.

If, in the past, educational research had shown itself capable of making serious advances in a reputable subject, this free-for-all might not now exist. But it has not. Nearly all of it can now be seen as resting on a doctrinaire and inappropriate methodology; and it is quite right that its proper procedures should now be under dispute. It is, however, quite wrong to suppose that such a dispute can be conducted sensibly by turning it into a competitive game of advertising or politics. This is not an issue for 'democratic procedures' or a 'general consensus'. It is as if a society, having seen astrology and alchemy to be misconceived, were to try to establish proper scientific procedures by inviting local dignitaries and leading artisans to sit on committees; or as if, having seen through the practices of witch-doctors, it were to hold numerous conferences of ex-witch-doctors and their patients in order to determine what ought to be done.

Who, then, should be seen as the appropriate experts or authorities? That is to say: who, in our present state of ignorance and muddle, should we chiefly rely on as guides towards intellectually respectable, practically useful and politically uncorrupted educational research? There is room for argument here; but one class of people are plainly excluded — those who have political axes to grind or those who see themselves as their servants. We require people who are primarily concerned with truth: not with what governments, or LEAs, or the Schools Council, or parents, or pupils, or any other body happen to find acceptable. Despite the BF, truth has nothing to do with contemporary acceptability; it is the failure to recognise and act on this rather obvious point that ultimately causes the corruption.

Since education is such a difficult subject, it is fairly clear that only a long-term or permanently established team of first-rate people has much hope of success in most areas; short-term and second-rate projects are virtually useless. It is also fairly plain that our methodological incompetence requires the services of a philosopher, and that practised and experienced teachers who are masters of their subject may have as much to tell us as the psychologist or the sociologist. But the crucial point is that such a team must be no more beholden to political pressures than are, say, research fellows of an Oxbridge college. The establishment of such teams might be at least a starting-point, even though (since practically nothing is known about education) many years' work lies ahead. Whether those who hold the power and the purse-strings are honest, sane and brave enough to relinquish some of their authority to such people is, of course, more doubtful; but to attempt any treatment of the fantasies of politicians and other such power-holders is beyond the scope even of this book.

'Empirical facts'

Conjoined with the myth about 'values', but perhaps more obviously liable to the BF than to the RF, is the idea that educational research — whatever else it may be — is about 'empirical facts'. It is, as we have seen, certainly not *only* about empirical facts; but the picture is apt to prevail that, once we have sorted out any purely conceptual or philosophical complexities, we can then get on with looking at 'the data', in the manner of the physicist or other natural scientist. But this is not so; though it is not easy to see just what we ought to say instead.

I begin with some informal remarks, not much above the level of common sense, about two common research techniques: the questionnaire and the search for 'replicability'. Asking people why they do things, even in a formal questionnaire, is less grotesquely behaviouristic than measuring movements or stimuli; but it is tarred with the same brush. An example: several researchers have published detailed statistics on the percentages of parents, teachers and others who approve or disapprove of 'RE' and 'moral education'. Any sensible person will at once wonder what it is that they are asked to approve or disapprove under these titles: might not different respondents mean different things by 'RE'? This turns out to be the case, as my colleagues and I found in some (unpublished) research at Oxford in 1970-71. 'Unstructured interviews in depth' (a grand name for just talking to people) showed quite clearly that different people had very different, and often diametrically opposed, concepts or pictures sparked off by 'RE', 'moral education' and other such terms. Hence the respondents were, in effect, being asked totally different questions. A lurid sub-example: respondents A and B both said they approved of 'sex education' in schools. Cross-questioned, A turned out to have a picture of 'sex education' in which the idea was essentially to repress pupils, 'keep them pure', etc., which A thought was a good idea; B turned out to have a 'permissive' or D. H. Lawrence-like picture of it, whereby kids were encouraged to have all sorts of sexual experience ('After all, that's education isn't it?'), which B thought was a good idea.

So obviously we have to find out the respondents' interpretations of any terms we use in a questionnaire. This is often extremely difficult, and involves — something missing from almost all psychological research — producing an adequate taxonomy of possible interpretations to begin with; and this in turn involves a lot of hard, not to say philosophical, thinking on our part. Things get worse when we ask respondents, for instance, why they chose to do this or that. We want to ensure that their answers are honest (difficult but not impossible), and also that they are giving their real reasons, not those that they have deceived themselves into accepting as their reasons (impossible by questionnaire methods only).

The only answer is to accept research methods that are not structured in this way. The myth is that this must result in 'soft' facts, mere 'subjective' impressions, etc.; but there are, of course, extremely rigid standards of procedure in this kind of research — as clinical psychologists, anthropologists and other workers who try to find out what is really going on in a person's head very well know. We might then have some chance of designing questionnaires that tell us something interesting about people.

Also borrowed from the physical sciences, with the disastrous inappropriateness typical of such borrowings, is the notion that any genuine or reputable piece of research must be 'replicable'. In one sense this notion is harmless. Any explanation is of the general form 'X behaved in way Y because of P and Q'; and any explainer thereby commits himself to the opinion that, other things being equal, P and Q will on any occasion make X behave in way Y. This sort of 'replicability' is part of the concept of an explanation.

Naturally we try to keep 'other things' as equal as possible (some call this 'controlling the variables'); but even in the physical sciences a total replication of any situation is virtually impossible. Yet much work has been done without this: consider astronomy, zoology and many other branches of science. What we do, of course, is to develop a refined picture of the field — planets, animals, or whatever it may be — in which we guess ('hypothesise') what the relevant factors are: colour and size are discounted, mass and skeletal structure seen to be relevant. We can get a long way in determining 'generative mechanisms' without anything like an *experimentum crucis* or total replicability. To put it another way: we could not get a proper idea of what 'other things being equal' meant in particluar contexts — of which 'other things' were relevant and which irrelevant — if we did not first fight our way towards a fairly high level of understanding.

A fortiori this is true of the human sciences. The notion of replicability in anthropology, for instance, is plainly absurd; yet equally plainly what the anthropologist learns about one tribe may help our understanding of tribes in general — just as (a point one might well have remembered right at the start) it is only by knowing some people that, in our everyday life, we come to have more general knowledge of people as a whole — without any question of replicated experiments. The same is true of the historian and the clinical psychiatrist.

The temptation, I think, is to insist on some particular concept of replicability ('Will it work with any children? With any teacher?'), and then to tailor our research interest to fit this model. Not surprisingly, there are few exciting results. What we should rather do is to ask the difficult but important questions, and tailor our research methods (including some concept of replicability, if you like) to fit these. To try to make psychology like physics is not the only defence against bias, prejudice or lack of rigour.

Can we gain a little more clarity and depth of perspective about just how the 'empirical facts' are modified by other considerations? A great deal has been written by philosophers of mind on this and cognate topics; but for our purposes the clearest way to make the relevant points, perhaps particularly for those not practised in philosophy, may be by offering in the first place an extended example. I give below the substance of a tape-recorded conversation, suitably edited, that I had with a PhD student. He was in the middle of research covering the general field of 'creative writing'; more particularly, he was concerned with teachers' opinions of 'creative writing' and the criteria by which they graded poems that their pupils were asked to write. He conceived this, in the orthodox manner, as a purely empirical study, designed primarily to find out 'the facts'. There were several stages in the conversation, which I mark in what follows.

Stage (1)

JBW: Surely if your research is going to be of any *educational use* or value, you must start with a clear idea of some justifiable educational objectives in the area of 'creative writing', and show why they're justifiable. Then the empirical work you do will be very useful, since (I take it) this work will show us how to achieve these objectives.

XY: No, I'll have to accept teachers' opinions on the objectives.

JBW: Buṫ those opinions might be wrong.

XY: Well, perhaps, but if there's a general consensus —

JBW: However general it was, they might still be wrong.

XY: All right, then: but at least I can do some straightforward empirical work about what teachers' opinions and practices actually *are*: and that will surely be useful to anyone interested in the field.

Stage (2)

JBW: I'm not really clear what *sort* of use, though. Quite a lot of their (or our) opinions and practices, in education and in other things, might be just the result of prejudice and fantasy; perhaps of interest to a psychiatrist or a historian of ideas, but what use would it be for *education*?

XY: Well, at least it might show us what these prejudices and fantasies were; then, if (as you say we ought to) we can get clear what 'creative writing' really should be about, we can have a better idea of what opposition to expect.

JBW: That sounds plausible, but I don't think it'll really do. It's rather like saying that research into (for instance) racial prejudice is useful, because it shows what people have what prejudices. But it can't show that in itself, not without some *prior* clarity about what's *reasonable* in this area. In other words, it's only if we *already* have a proper notion of what counts as being unprejudiced, or sane, or reasonable, or whatever words we should use, in relation to other races — in fact, to other people with different characteristics from ourselves in general — that we can *identify* cases as cases of *prejudice*. Without that prior idea, we wouldn't know where to start.

XY: I don't get that.

JBW: Maybe I should have used a better example. Well, suppose you were doing research on 'failure in mathematics', or something like that. Then you wouldn't know *what* to do research *on*, what to *identify* as 'failure', unless you were already clear about what it was to do mathematics properly or successfully. So if you're arguing that it's useful to know what these people think, just to be able to identify the opposition, then that argument already assumes that we know what it's opposition *to*. I mean, suppose we got properly clear about 'creative writing', and said that its value was ABC, and that it ought to be graded in ways PQR, taught by methods XYZ, and so on. *Then* you could find out what teachers thought, and then you could see how far it was 'opposition', or agreement, or just muddle. You'd say, for instance, 'They've got the point about A and B, but they've missed C, and so instead of PQR they grade the poems by STU, and teach it by methods VW'.

Stage (3)

XY: Very well, I'll lower my sights and just say that — without any particular reference to education at all, if you like, or anyway without any intention of trying to *improve* it — all I'm trying to do is to find out what teachers think and do about 'creative writing'. It's just a straightforward empirical study of certain opinions and practices in schools. Surely I don't *still* need a clear idea beforehand of what it's reasonable to think about it.

JBW: Well, that's more difficult. But there seems to be one problem, anyway: that is, how are you to tell it's really *creative writing* they're thinking about?

XY: But surely, they use the phrase 'creative writing' and say and do things in connection with that phrase. What more do you want?

JBW: Supposing they mean different things by the phrase? Or supposing they aren't really clear what they do mean by it? Then you can say, in your doctoral thesis, 'These are teachers' views about creative writing'; but *are* they?

XY: They must be, mustn't they, since that's what they say their own views are about?

JBW: No, there's a muddle in that. I mean, suppose we were finding out people's views on Communism: and suppose one person when using the word 'Communism' had in mind the pure doctrines of Marx or Engels, and another had in mind the share-and-share-alike practices of the early Christians, and another the actual set-up of the USSR, and another China, and so on. Then they'd clearly be giving you views on different things. So you'd have first to decide what *you* meant, or what you thought it was reasonable to mean, by 'Communism', and *then* (only then) could you know whether their views were *relevant* or not. And similarly if you're interested in whether they 'value' creative writing, or why they value it, and what they do in practice about it.

Stage (4)

XY: All right, I'll lower my sights still further. I don't need to say that this research *is* actually about creative writing; I can simply say that the information I collect is what the phrase 'creative writing' (and a number of specific questions about it) actually sparks off from teachers. I could call it 'Teachers' Reactions to the Idea of Creative Writing', or something like that. Surely at least I can collect empirical information about their states of mind and opinions and so forth, without having to do any of this conceptual analysis stuff beforehand.

JBW: Well, there are difficulties even about that. You can't talk of collecting 'empirical information', or 'reactions', as if they were like pebbles lying around; human behaviour isn't like that. You have to be able to *identify* it, and you can only identify it by the sort of empathetic process various philosophers have written about — you have to know what game they're playing. You can't just photograph it, because what they overtly do is tied up with their intentions and purposes and so on. You have to find out what's going on in their heads.

XY: Oh, yes, I know all about that, it's all that stuff in Peter Winch and so forth. You mean I should go about it more like an anthropologist or a historian or a clinical psychiatrist. Certainly. But isn't that still a straightforwardly empirical business? Where does the philosophy come in?

Stage (5)

JBW: I'm not sure whether 'philosophy' is the right word. Certainly making sense of what people think and do involves making sense of what they *say* — in public or to themselves; and that certainly overlaps a lot with what Austin called 'linguistic phenomenology', and Austin is normally counted as a philosopher.

XY: Yes, but it's also a matter of whether they mean what they say, and of what they actually do; and surely, anyway, we're not just doing 'linguistic phenomenology' in the abstract, so to speak, with imaginary cases and borderline cases and all the other Austinian techniques — we're saying something about particular people and particular times, and producing truths about them which could be otherwise; so that they must be empirical or contingent truths, not the conceptual or necessary truths that philosophers go in for.

JBW: That's perfectly true, and of course I'm not trying to say that there isn't such a thing as empirical work. I think what I'm trying to say is that it can't be *just* empirical; or rather, that any empirical work relies on an initial clarity about concepts and values, and perhaps particularly about motives.

XY: Sorry, I don't follow you.

JBW: Well, I'm not quite sure what I want to say. Suppose we take an example. For instance, some of your English-teachers will say that making children write poems is a good thing because it increases creativity, and doesn't force them necessarily into having to write in sonnet form which would be very authoritarian, and encourages them to be authentic, and so on. Now what you have, empirically, is the *words* — 'creative', 'authoritarian', 'authentic'; but how do you make sense of these just by empirical techniques? No doubt they represent some kind of facts, but *what* facts?

XY: I suppose you could ask them what they meant, and that would show what facts.

JBW: But suppose they *didn't know* what they meant? Or suppose they meant, or seemed to mean, something that wasn't really intelligible at all? For instance, a man might *tell* you that by being against 'authoritarian' teaching he meant that schools shouldn't have any rules, teachers shouldn't be authorities in any sense at all, and whatever the children learned shouldn't be governed by any kind of standards. But this is just incoherent as it stands: contradictory, indeed. 'Learn' just does logically imply 'standards', just as any institution implies rules and authorities. So how could we make any sense of it?

XY: Well, all right, how could we? But people do, surely. I mean, psychiatrists and so on aren't philosophers, but they make sense of even the weirdest cases.

JBW: Yes, but this is only possible against a background of intelligible human interests: psychiatrists attach weird behaviour to these (sadism to the desire for power, being a miser to the desire for security, and so on). If they couldn't make this sort of attachment or see what sort of good (what *species boni*) their patients were aiming at, they couldn't explain or cure.

XY: But isn't that an empirical matter? I mean, determining what actually *are* human interests? These English-teachers and psychiatric patients and so on may be muddled in what they say, but isn't what they want just a matter of fact?

JBW: Not *just* a matter of fact. Quite a few philosophers have argued that you can't want just *anything*: that there's a standard stock of reasons or motives, as you might say, to one or the other of which you have to refer what people do if it's to make sense. And I don't think all of these — perhaps none of them — are empirical: if by that you mean just contingent interests that might be otherwise. How could any creature, even a Martian, *not* want power or security? Of course it's an empirical question why this chap who's a sadist or that chap who's a miser seeks these (inevitable) goals in these contingently peculiar and unnecessary ways. But you need the background of standard interests to start with.

Professional philosophers will have no difficulty in recognising some of these points, made here in casual conversation; but it may be helpful to classify them in relation to educational research. The five stages of the argument above amount to the points:

(1) That if a piece of research is to be of any direct educational use, its topic or title — 'creative writing', 'critical thinking', 'success in learning science', or anything else — has to be expanded and translated in such a way as (a) to make clear what *counts as* 'creative writing' (or whatever), and (b) to show the kind of good, or advantage or educational benefit that it is supposed to produce.

(2) That we cannot, just by empirical methods, 'identify the opposition' to any educational good until we are clear about the good in the first place.

(3) That we cannot even canvass opinions on X unless both we and the research subjects are clear about what counts as X.

(4)   That we cannot even identify the opinions or states of mind (whether or not about X) of research subjects unless we are able to understand the logic of those states: the logic of 'what game they're playing'.

(5)   Understanding this logic is not a purely empirical matter, since it will only make sense in reference to a (conceptually derived) set of standard interests.

It is, I think, tolerably clear that nearly all past and present educational research is not based on a proper grasp of these points. Fortunately some (not much) of such research has proceeded in conjunction with some tacit understanding of them: one might say, common sense has broken through on occasion; and this means that some interesting and useful work has been done. But it has been done against heavy odds; and if we can offer any alternative procedures that would incorporate these points, or at least not fall foul of them, a great deal would surely be gained.

The trouble with talking about 'alternative procedures', however, is that people will expect some kind of semi-algorithmic 'methodology', analogous to the orthodox methodology of the natural and behavioural sciences; whereas the truth is that the relevant procedures are in essence fairly simple, and governed more by standards than by cut-and-dried rules. The phrase 'in essence' covers, of course, a multitude of sins and virtues: nobody supposes that it is easy to be a good philosopher, or phenomenologist or psychiatrist. But the kind of difficulties that these disciplines face is essentially different from those that educational researchers, in the orthodox tradition, usually construe themselves as facing.

As with the 'value-free' myth, this too has (in a broad sense) political implications. Perhaps the most important thing is that educational researchers — and this applies, I regret to say, also to those in positions of power and influence who organise or supervise such research — should be forced to recognise a basic challenge right at the start. Not much, initially, is gained by trying to explain to them the alternative procedures in full (which would, anyway, amount to giving them some quite sophisticated grasp of philosophy), or by those — very few — philosophers who have anything to do with educational research trying to fight for a fair slice of the cake or a fair crack of the whip. But at least we may be able to make researchers recognise that some of their sacred cows can be slaughtered without loss, thereby perhaps making space for more hard-working animals.

The sacred cows I have in mind are, again, not mistaken beliefs about procedure and methodology at a sophisticated level. Few educational researchers are sophisticated in regard to *any* procedure and methodology: most of them, quite understandably, tend to follow prevailing orthodoxy or semi-political pressures in a deferential fashion. But they are, I think, slightly more amenable to rational discussion when it comes to making judgements, not so much about the sophisticated methodology of research, but about its prior organisation and some fairly straightforward issues in its administration. Two briefly sketched examples of this may be helpful.

First, there is the dominating idea that researchers should 'narrow the scope' of their research, or 'circumscribe' it along orthodox lines (ultimately derived from the natural sciences): for instance, not 'creative writing' but perhaps 'the views of Oxfordshire teachers on creative writing for 11-year-old children in selected schools'. This idea effectively inhibits the kind of general or conceptual considerations that, as we have seen, must be got straight *before* any 'narrow' empirical work of this kind can make sense. Similarly a topic such as 'The aims of teaching modern languages' is too alarming for most research students and supervisors, because they cannot see (since they do not understand) the importance of gaining a general conceptual grasp of such aims. So such a topic might be reduced to, say, 'Aims and objectives in teaching French to primary school children' — and even this would be chiefly a matter of gaining empirical information: what working-parties of primary school teachers had said, what might be needed for a united Europe, and so on.

Secondly, there is the idea that we must *first* identify a research area and *then* hire researchers to investigate it, after having described the area in some detail, explained how the research is to be done and how long it will take, and in general 'made a case' (usually to some funding body) for doing the work. The fallacy here, of course, is to suppose that these supposedly simple and prior tasks of identifying and explaining are not themselves *part of* the research: indeed its most important part. (As if it were a matter of common sense, or practical politics, to get that sort of work properly done, when in fact it is just here that the intellectual and conceptual sophistication is required). The correct procedure, obviously enough, is *first* to get highly competent people, perhaps give them some roughly outlined research title, and then to let *them* define the scope and nature of the research. Mistakes in this procedure also proceed ultimately from the idea that there are easily identifiable 'problems' or regrettable 'facts' — rather as if we were talking about specific and easily seen diseases, like cancer or influenza — which, having identified (by asking teachers, or politicians, or whoever), we can then hire empirical researchers to explain and perhaps cure.

My impression is, perhaps optimistically, that the younger generation of researchers (possibly for bad reasons, connected with a general dislike of authority and orthodoxy) is less liable to these *idées fixes*, and hence in principle more able and willing to do something more sensible. I have known several students who, not regarding these cows as sacred and relying on a rugged independence and common sense, have in effect *taught themselves*, or arranged for themselves to be taught, enough 'philosophy' or conceptual competence for their actual research to be coherent and educationally valuable. Usually they have done this in the teeth of opposition from empirically minded supervisors, fear about the eventual success of their PhD theses, and a good deal of personal anxiety; but at least they have done it.

This is perhaps unsurprising, since young people, though often wilder or dottier than their elders, are at least less likely to have been totally corrupted by some orthodoxy. It suggests, at least, the correct point of entry for those who hope for rational change. We have first to establish, not the sophisticated kind of understanding about basic methodology (which most people will simply not grasp), but acceptance of the general principle that there *are* what may loosely be called 'conceptual difficulties' in almost all educational research; so that research students and others may, at least, pass through the hands of those who are conceptually competent — or, if not that, be allowed the right to raise conceptual doubts and questions that they can themselves pursue with the aid of the philosophical literature and anyone they can find to help them. I should be inclined *not* to try, or not to try too hard, to spell out to the layman just what these 'conceptual difficulties' are, at least to begin with; that simply confuses them and creates an atmosphere of distrust. But they can, with care, be brought to accept some organisation of research that allows these difficulties to surface and creates some (however small) institutional arrangements for dealing with them — if, that is, the controlling fantasies can be kept at bay.

Practical implementation

I conclude with a few remarks on this topic, to give some idea of how constantly important fantasy is in educational research, even if we succeed in making something respectable out of it.

It is fairly clear from most discussions of this topic that we are dominated by the ideas (i) that educational researchers have discovered things and produced 'findings' that incorporate truths (a) not already known or easily found out by people of ordinary common sense and imagination, (b) demonstrably relevant to indisputable educational objectives, and (c) able in principle to be used to advantage by teachers, parents and others; (ii) that the practical implementation of these 'findings' must consist of teaching people these truths and helping them to translate their force into practical methods. It is as if scientists had discovered new and more effective techniques relevant to building bridges or curing rheumatism, techniques that needed to be understood by bridge-builders and doctors and translated into practical forms.

In most cases — I do not say all — the assumptions in (i) above are, as I have tried to show elsewhere, clearly false (J. Wilson, 1972a). This does not mean that educationalists and researchers may not have true and important things to say to teachers and parents; nor that such things are totally obvious — it may, indeed, require 'research' to see them clearly; nor that some kind of work is not needed in getting them to bear on educational practice — that teachers and parents will immediately see the force of them for themselves. Indeed, this last point gives the game away: if the position were analogous to bridge-building and medicine, new 'findings' *would* be very easily and quickly assimilated into practice. It would be like handing people, who already knew what they wanted to do, a better (quicker, cheaper) method of doing it. The implication is that we must look for new and different pictures of what it is to 'implement research findings'.

We have already seen how any interpretation of 'research' that assimilates educational research to the natural sciences (along with psychology and sociology), and any interpretation of 'findings' analogous to those of the natural sciences — say, the discovery of a new drug or a quicker technique for extracting iron from ore — leads at once to disaster. Until we get free of this idea, we cannot make progress. When we are free of it, we have still to resist the temptation of using some *one* model of our situation, based on an over-simple distinction between whether something is 'known' or 'not known' by teachers, parents, local administrators, politicians, etc. The position is far more complicated than that. What complicates it is not, or not only, the 'variables' applying to the clientèle — whether the teachers are well read, the parents anxious to do their best, and so on — but rather the nature of the truths we need to impress on them.

My contention, made here in the teeth of the BF, is that many of such truths, far from being specialised and sophisticated empirical truths (as, for instance, are the truths of physics and chemistry), are either straightforwardly *conceptual* or else so deeply empirical as to flow rather from prolonged reflection on the nature of human beings, the objectives of learning, etc. than from anything properly to be called scientific experiment. What is it for a class to be 'well disciplined', and why is this essential for learning? What are we to mean by 'learning to read'? Why is it important for children to be loved? Why do institutions have to have rules, and rules punishments? Why can certain decisions about children only be properly taken by those who know them intimately? Pursuit of these and many other questions does, indeed, produce important truths — obvious, perhaps, to those who have pursued them properly, but not in the same way obvious, nor having the same sort of force, to those who have not.

A few possibilities here are:

(1) There is the person who (often, I fear, because he has been brainwashed by current fashion or even educational research itself) would initially want to deny some truth: for instance, that being well-*disciplined* has to do with *obedience* (not just with being trouble-free), or that *rules* (rather than just wishes or pious hopes) necessarily involve *punishments*. 'Implementing research findings' here would have to mean, first of all, getting him to see the reasons why these truths are true.

(2) There is the person who in a way 'knows' these truths to be true, but only (so to speak) if and when he keeps his head. We all know, in our saner moments, that having lots of money and status and fast cars does not, by and large, make people happy; but we lose our heads and forget this, both in reference to ourselves and when making educational arrangements. We know what rules are

required, more or less, for the effective running of any educational institution; but we forget this, or lose our nerve, when we face actual situations. Here the task must be to give people a *secure* and *permanent* grasp of the truths, in defiance of fantasy.

(3) There is the person who, perhaps through lack of imagination or reflection, has some sort of permanent knowledge of the truths, but fails to feel their full force and implications. We might all know, and always agree, that (say) love is more important than social status; but we might see this more as a calendar motto than a fully fledged and glowingly important truth. We might not have reflected sufficiently on what 'love' implies, or what love is, or why it is important, or what happens when it is absent. Here we have somehow to sophisticate and strengthen the imagination of those to whom we are selling this truth.

(4) There is the person who accepts the truth fully, but cannot do much about it. This is for a variety of reasons: he may simply be too weak-willed, or have insufficient time or resources, or lack knowledge of the particular techniques required to implement it. Only in the latter case can we apply the model I have been criticising: if the objective is clear and properly understood *by the teacher* (parent, etc.), and if the researcher has proved that a particular technique or piece of hardware will achieve it more efficiently than others, then of course he can say so — and the teacher will adopt it willingly. Indeed, he would no doubt seek it out for himself. But there are, I think, very few cases of this kind. Such cases as there are tend, unsurprisingly, to operate at a fairly low level: one overhead projector is better than another, one sort of blackboard easier to clean, and so on.

On the understanding that these possibilities are not exhaustive, and that our first task ought to consist of adding to and clarifying them, can anything helpful be said about what 'implementing research findings' might — on this revised picture — actually look like? Well, one thing is both clear and important: the *manner in which* such truths can be properly brought home to people will not look anything like the issuing of recipes, or a set of empirical 'proofs' that X works better than Y, or the publication of new formulae. This will work for simple empirical truths, but not for these. Nor, again, will it look much like a publicity exercise. I do not deny that, as a starter, it may be useful to gain initial attention if (for instance) we run some sort of advertising campaign to make people start thinking about, say, the importance of love or discipline or language. But (a) such campaigns cannot keep up a full head of steam for long; and, more importantly, (b) publicity alone cannot *teach* anybody anything. The weaknesses noted above in (1)—(4) are such that the person needs to learn, not merely to be reminded.

In what sort of context or manner, then, do people learn such things? Much will of course depend on the sophistication of the clientèle. There are people for whom books, and the written word generally, are pedagogically powerful; whose daily lives and perceptions — even, perhaps, when teaching 3C on a Friday afternoon — are permanently changed by literature that spells out or incorporates these truths. We think here most naturally of philosophical writing on the one hand, and imaginative or fictional writing on the other — with, of course, a broad borderline in between (in which one might want to put a good deal of psychoanalytic literature, a good many religious documents and a lot of 'philosophy' that professional philosophers might reject as such). It is these forms, if any, that are tailored to fit the messages we are talking about. But how many people are there, in fact, whose appreciation of (say) love is in fact permanently enriched by (say) Plato's *Symposium*, or even Tolstoy's novels? Our audience is not so sophisticated, even if we (as 'researchers' or 'implementers') ourselves are.

Naturally other media spring to mind: most obviously, perhaps, the film or the video-tape; and, even though one might be worried about whether the audience were really getting the point (rather than just having a good time) without a clearer, and necessarily more verbal, spelling-out of what the point was, researchers will rightly not turn up their noses at such techniques. But they would, I suspect, rapidly come to feel that the really important thing is a *closely knit context* of discussion: a group of people who can trust each other sufficiently, and have sufficiently good communication with each other, to make some progress in the relevant kinds of understanding.

It is, of course, fashionable to stress the 'gulf' between 'researchers' and 'teachers'; but this is usually presented as regrettable either because the separation causes envy and distrust, or because it puts each party out of touch with the other. Such a presentation is not so much mistaken as superficial: for it would apply equally to (say) doctors and professors of medicine, or to pharmacists and research chemists. In fact there are few complaints over these cases; and this is, again, because both parties know what their proper subject-matter is. Because they are clear about what counts as a proper and relevant 'research finding', they can (and do) organise effective methods of communication. The key point about educational research and its implementation is that the nature of the subject, the kind of truths we are dealing with, itself involves closely organised discussion — *not*, or at least nothing like so much, lengthy empirical collections of data, giant theses written up in an elaborate form, and so on.

We need, to begin with, small groups of researchers who will themselves be able to create and profit from such a context; and who will, above all, be able to *establish* truth or clarity in some educational topic. 'Implementation' is then largely a matter of bringing in teachers, parents, etc. so that they may be initiated into the ground that has been gained. The danger of describing this as 'getting teachers to join in the dialogue' or 'contribute to the discussion', or whatever, is that we may come to believe that there are no such things as truths or right answers in this business — or that, if there are, they must be 'empirical' or 'matters of fact'. In our saner moments we know this to be false, but we often act and talk as if it were true.

Secondly, because of the lack of the right kind of sophistication mentioned earlier — and this is as likely to apply to the researchers as to teachers — we need to make quite sure that what we *do* know (if only, as I put it, 'in our saner moments') does not diminish or disappear. This means, above all, keeping our feet on the ground; and this, in turn, means eschewing jargon and most of what passes for 'educational theory', speaking plain English and putting clarity before anything else. We come back, rapidly and obviously enough, to where we began — to the need to understand and control our fantasies.

CHAPTER 6

The Preparation of Teachers

I shall deal fairly briefly with this topic, partly because I have written about it more extensively elsewhere (J. Wilson, 1975) and partly because the central points are (from a strictly intellectual viewpoint) more than usually obvious, requiring comparatively little philosophical analysis. But the way in which the fantasies — particularly the BF — operate here merits our particular attention, since current practice and discussions of the topic illustrate how apparently contradictory views and régimes may all be dominated by the same kind of bewitchment. A brief historical sketch might look like this:

(1) Some years ago it was believed that there was something called 'educational theory' — perhaps a kind of mixture or amalgam of philosophy, psychology and sociology of education — which all intending teachers needed to know, and which formed a solid body of knowledge on which practical teaching could be firmly based; rather as the theories of science (mechanics, biology, etc.) provided a basis for the practice of engineers and doctors. So a good many professors of these subjects were appointed, and student-teachers had to listen to lectures and pass examinations in them.

(2) More recently people have begun to question either the existence of this corpus of knowledge or its relevance to practical teaching. 'Being a good teacher' is construed as essentially a 'practical' matter, to which perhaps no 'theory' is of great importance. So (the story goes) the training of teachers — and here 'training' would be more appropriate than 'education' — should be construed practically, on something like an apprentice model: the intending

teacher needs plenty of down-to-earth experience of the classroom under the guidance of an experienced practising teacher or 'professional tutor', and some general 'initiation into the system' of education as it now is. His preparation should be 'school-based' and not 'theory-based'.

Both these views share the assumption that being a good teacher is wholly or primarily a matter of practising some kind of *craft*. Perhaps it is a rather esoteric craft, for the successful practice of which we need 'theory' (as motor mechanics need to know about the internal combustion engine) rather than just common sense; or perhaps it is a fairly pedestrian, down-to-earth sort of craft, for which we need practical experience (as potters or wheelwrights need chiefly to gain experience as apprentices, without the benefit of much theory). Perhaps, indeed, as is commonly believed in some educational circles, the idea of being a good teacher can be reduced to a set of 'teaching skills' that we can train students to master. The implicit analogy is with those jobs or crafts that are chiefly a matter of what we might call *technical ability* or *professional competence*: being a doctor or nurse or engineer, knowing how to sail a boat or look after horses or make pots.

Now of course to *some* extent this is true: there are certain practical or technical aspects of any teacher's job that are very important and that, being practical or technical, can only be learned in the ways described above — either by applying knowledge derived from some set of theoretical rules, and/or by practical experience in the classroom. But it is abundantly clear that these are not the only, or the most important, aspects of 'being a good teacher'. If we think of other analogies — being a good priest, or parent, or psychotherapist, or social worker, or youth leader — we can see that the crucial qualities do not lie in that dimension at all. Even the idea of being the sort of person who is good at encouraging an interest in learning, who inspires students with his enthusiasm or who communicates knowledge and understanding effectively, is not to be translated in terms of *technical* qualities. Where we are dealing with a fairly cut-and-dried enterprise, in which technical and practical ability rather than more personal qualities and attitudes is of paramount importance, we talk readily and correctly of 'competence': we want competent doctors, engineers and so on. But do we want 'competent' parents, priests and social workers? Well, of course we do not want incompetent ones; but (we feel) it is not primarily a matter of competence.

If we ask ourselves what it is a matter of, we find that we cannot even approach the question seriously without throwing over both the BF and the RF. We could say, vaguely, that good teachers (parents, etc.) have certain attributes not easy to assess and impossible to reduce to any set of 'skills': they are keen on their subject and have a strong desire that others should be keen also; they understand and care for their pupils; they are not afraid to maintain discipline; they are tolerably sane and secure people; they have a sense of humour; and they are not crippled by doctrinaire fantasies about education. These qualities are mostly a matter of attitude, not of 'skills' at all.

All this (I submit) we *know perfectly well already*. The difficulty, as usual psychological rather than intellectual, is that we do not have a very clear idea about how to train or educate intending teachers with respect to these attributes. Hence the temptation either to deny the existence of the attributes (the RF) or to regress to the BF, which allows us to concentrate solely on attributes ('skills'), which are easier to manage. ('But how are we to *measure* a student-teacher's keenness on his subject, or understanding of pupils, or psychological security?') We resign ourselves to a view of 'being a good teacher', and a consequent view of teacher-education that is less worrying: perhaps an approach in terms of 'behavioural objectives', perhaps one in terms of 'theoretical knowledge' — anything, so long as it is visible, reasonably cut-and-dried, and sufficiently simple-minded.

In fact, once we are willing to face the questions, we fairly soon become a little more confident about answering them. There are, quite evidently, *some* things that we can do or try to do with intending teachers that are relevant to the centrally important attributes: things for which 'philosophy' and 'psychotherapy' would be grand and misleading names, but which would at least represent a serious attempt to get the students to understand themselves and their fantasies a little more deeply, and perhaps exercise a little more control over them. I have discussed this at length elsewhere (J. Wilson, 1975); here I wish only to make the point that some such attempt seems logically required if we are to take the preparation of teachers seriously.

We may usefully generalise from this and other cases, and notice that the whole way of thinking that distinguishes 'theory' and 'practice' in such cases seems to be tarred with the BF brush. This way of thinking fits the cut-and-dried examples, or what one might call the strictly empirical areas where words like 'fact', 'competence', 'skill' and others are in place. Of course there are many such areas, though perhaps fewer than we like to think, since a great many enterprises depend not only on competence but on attitude. There would be something important missing — important not only generally, but for the actual enterprise of medicine or curing — if doctors and nurses in hospitals were replaced by (more competent) robots; even, or perhaps particularly, if janitors and tea-ladies were replaced by computerised cleaners and coffee-machines. And in other enterprises, as with teaching, 'competence' labels a comparatively unimportant dimension. We do not, primarily, want *competent* lovers, husbands, sons, friends, etc.

Sexual relationships offer a perennially topical example. Just as the RF implicitly denies *any* 'right' or 'wrong' in such relationships, so the BF tempts us to suppose that sex may be treated as a technical matter. If we study it earnestly in this light, we may begin (sensibly enough) by talking about biological 'theory' and its implications for 'practice'; and then perhaps move on to some 'theory' in social psychology, which will generate 'practical' implications — the 'social skills' of a 'competent' lover or mistress, to be deployed when dating or courting or in bed. But one does not have to hold very high-minded views about sex to recognise that it is not a sport or a series of gymnastic exercises or a conventionalised tea-party: it has something to do with human feelings and emotions, not just with physical movements or social rituals. Even in its most down-to-earth cases there are visible signs of aggression, or loneliness, or fear, or vulnerability, or (one might hope) affection. If (which is doubtful) we can talk without misleading of 'being good at sex' ('good in bed'), the relevant attributes escape the restrictions of the BF.

Fortunately sex is sufficiently powerful to break such bonds in most people's minds. Less visibly absurd, if also less important, are the innumerable cases where the BF causes us to erect a 'theory' and 'practice' of a grandiose and inflated kind that does not fit the actual enterprise. Thus there is, of course, such a thing as being a good air hostess (receptionist, child-minder, etc.); but we do not necessarily produce better ones by giving them a four-year degree course in 'Aeroplane Administration' if such a course fails to concentrate on what the intending air hostess is *like*, what sort of *person* she is. This is not a matter of 'theory'; nor is it a matter of 'practice', if that is to mean practice in going through a set of ritual motions supposed to be beneficial — the artificial smile, the quiet impersonal voice, the ritual remarks ('Welcome aboard', 'Thank you for travelling with us today', and so on). In anything like a human relationship, the theory-practice distinction and the BF on which it is based produces only what is demonstrably phoney and insincere.

Let us see if we can be a little clearer and more precise about teacher-training. There seems to be three models to which we are tempted to assimilate the preparation of teachers, or in terms of which we construe the meaning of 'a good teacher':

(a) *Saints and Heroes.* This is an old, certainly nowadays an old-fashioned, model. In historical or high-minded moods, one might connect 'a good teacher' with the idea of some saint-like or heroic figure with semi-magical or at least non-negotiable qualities ('inspiration', etc.): Socrates, Jesus, Abelard, Thomas Arnold, and so on. The implications of this model for teacher-training are tolerably clear: they are nil. 'Teachers are born and not made.'

(b) *Drivers and Potters.* This model, at the other extreme, regards being a teacher as some kind of art or craft, a low-level *techne*, a matter of what can properly be called *skill* or a set of skills: learning it is rather like learning to drive or make pots or ride horses or do woodwork. Little or no 'theory' is relevant: it is a matter of aptitude plus practical experience. The implication is that practical experience, plus some guidance or 'monitoring' of the experience and some fairly hard and non-controversial knowledge of the prevailing system (how the traffic works, how the stables are run), is the only or at least the most important method of preparation.

(c) *Doctors and Engineers.* This slightly more sophisticated, though equally improper, model is perhaps the most popular today. Some sort of distinction is made between 'theory' and 'practice': the would-be doctor or engineer needs an adequate theoretical understanding of a branch of science (medicine, mechanics, or whatever), plus the practical experience required to apply it. Teachers — the story goes — similarly need a dose of 'theory' combined in some effective way with a dose or doses of 'practice'.

In current debates, or in changes of fashion, people tend either to stick firmly to one or other of these models, or else to change models when one becomes clearly absurd. Thus if you believe, as many do, that there is no solid body of 'theory' analogous to medical science or mechanics that all teachers need to know, then you come off model (c), and revert perhaps to (b): 'There's no proper theory, so it's all a matter of practice.' Then perhaps you face the obvious fact that there is more to it than just practice — that being a good teacher is not just a matter of 'competence' and 'skill'; and so revert to model (a), which allows one to say that skill is indeed not enough, but that what lies beyond is non-negotiable: 'All we can do is to give them practical experience and some guidance: the rest is a matter of their basic personalities, which we can't do anything about.'

The fact is that we know well enough, when we stop to think about it, that 'a good teacher' does not fit any of these models. Of course there is some truth in all of them. (a) Basic and unchangeable (untrainable, ineducable) qualities are important; (b) practical experience and competence are certainly *part* of being a good teacher; (c) there may even be *some* bits of knowledge that one could fairly call 'theoretical' and that teachers need to know. All this is not in dispute. But we have only to consider a few parallels, like 'a good parent', 'a good social worker', 'a good therapist', 'a good priest', 'a good youth leader', and so on, to appreciate that none of these models is central. Being a good parent is not just, nor even primarily, a matter of (a) saintliness and heroism, (b) practical competence, or (c) theoretical knowledge plus practical experience.

What then does constitute the good teacher? Or perhaps it is better to narrow the question slightly, and ask something like 'What are the causes of the kinds of major mistakes, whether of omission or commission, or the major defects, that teachers display and that we might be able to help them overcome?' A great deal turns here on giving a *correct description* of these; otherwise we shall find ourselves driven back to one or other of the false models, and describe them as 'a lack of inspiration', 'a lack of skill', or 'a lack of theoretical knowledge' — though we know well enough that when parents, for instance, go wrong their errors are not primarily due to any of these.

It is some help, if not much, to say that the most important defects concern the teacher's *attitudes*. Thus a teacher may have a very right-wing, or alternatively a very left-wing or 'liberationist', attitude to discipline and authority; to freedom and compulsion in education; to the kind of pastoral care or staff-pupil relationships that he thinks ought to exist. He may see his subject as primarily valuable for its 'usefulness' or 'social relevance', or for its individual enrichment and intrinsic worth; and this will, obviously enough, affect how he teaches it (even how, or whether, he uses the technology and 'hardware' connected with it). He may see his pupils primarily in terms of social class or Piagetian stages, or in terms of other categories that carry certain attitudes with them. His defects, or the mistakes he makes, will be largely a function of the irrationality of the attitudes.

Here it is very important to see that attitudes are not restricted to some one 'domain' ('cognitive', 'affective', etc.), and cannot be hived off under some single heading, such as 'the basic personality'. An attitude involves both a set of beliefs and a set of feelings (together with tendencies to act); and even this puts it badly, since — as philosophers have been trying to hammer into the heads of psychologists for at least thirty years — emotions involve, or are partly constituted by, beliefs. We have only to think of a few misguided attitudes (race prejudice, Fascism, weak-kneed liberalism, etc.) to see how they intertwine. The person has some *idée fixe*, some basic mental posture, some fantasy or connected set of unconscious ideas; and this involves both the acceptance of propositions that are, for empirical or even for strictly conceptual reasons, untenable and the acceptance of feelings which enshrine and reinforce them. Fear of one's own aggression may rationalise itself in a belief or fantasy about the importance of teachers never behaving firmly or authoritatively (never getting angry); fear of one's own impotence may rationalise itself into a 'spare the rod and spoil the child' fantasy. One does not have to accept specific psychoanalytic stories in order to see that attitudes are, as it were, a seamless web of thought and feeling.

If we now ask what can be done about this in the preparation of teachers, we must again avoid the bewitchment of particular models; models that are, unsurprisingly, either the same as or at least correlative to those mentioned earlier. I say 'unsurprisingly', because the psychological function of the models is, essentially, to make certain jobs and aspects of life easier. Being a good parent is difficult. Since it is primarily a matter of attitude — one might say, of being sane and loving as well as competent — and the only way forward is the rather murky and vague way marked by such terms as 'acquiring insight', 'coming to see one's prejudices', 'making sense of the problems', etc., we tend to relapse into construing it on some other model that saves us from pursuing this path. We find ourselves thinking that it is (a) a matter of being a saint or hero, (b) a matter of practical competence only, or (c) a matter of applying 'theory' to 'practice'. In just such a way, we have to avoid the idea that there is some *one* method of defending teachers against the wrong sort of attitude: that they will learn, for instance, *only* by being prodded into moral virtue by sermons, or only by habituating themselves into certain 'social skills', or only by absorbing psychological or sociological theory.

The use of particular examples, rather than some overall model, may help us. Suppose an intending teacher who is — to put it in the most general way — muddled or doctrinaire or neurotic or 'hung up' about authority and discipline. Then

(i) he will have certain views or *opinions* about these topics, which can be discussed and criticised philosophically;

(ii) he will have certain *feelings* or natural reactions, which can also be evoked and inspected (together with the underlying reasons for them);

(iii) he will tend to *act* in certain practical ways, and these actions can be monitored and discussed.

In other words, we can get at his general attitude in a very large number of ways. We have the possibility of philosophical discussion and stringently rational argument; of encouraging him to voice, read about, role-play or act out his feelings; of giving him different kinds of experience in educational situations that call for a proper use of authority, and showing him what happens if he does the wrong thing. There will be books, different kinds of conversations and different contexts of 'experience', all of which can make an effective contribution. It is not that, once we throw 'theory' overboard, we have left ourselves with too little to do; on the contrary, we have an *embarras de richesse*. But we only perceive what *richesse* if we first perceive clearly what we are trying to do.

Certain general points of method follow from this. First, we need to start from some set of topics or issues (though these words may make it seem too 'cognitive') that are demonstrably of importance, in the sense that teachers can go badly wrong in these areas. (There are plenty of candidates). We can then consider what mixture of methods — discussion, role-play, etc. — is likely to do most good in each case. Secondly, since this will clearly vary depending on the students concerned and is in any case a complex and delicate business, we need coherent working groups of students together with staff members, within which we can build up the degree of trust, communication and general understanding without which none of this is likely to get very far. Since many fantasies and 'hang-ups' in these areas are common to many people, mass lectures have some part to play: one may, for instance, outline and make real the kind of 'mental set' that weak-kneed liberals or insecure authoritarians are likely to find themselves saddled with. But most of the work, by its very nature, will probably need to be done in some kind of smaller group.

It is illusory to suppose that these points have no application within the student's own teaching subject. Some believe, or act as if they believe, that they affect only the 'general' work that the student is supposed to pursue in 'education' or 'educational theory'; and that his 'method' or 'curricular' work — what he is taught in reference to his particular subject — is, comparatively speaking, non-controversial. This is not so, and again betrays the influence of the false models mentioned earlier. Of course it is non-controversial (a) that some students have some sort of innate or at least non-negotiable qualities that make them 'inspired' teachers of X or Y; (b) that all students need those practical competences and experiences that will improve what can fairly be called 'skills' (most obviously, knowledge of resources and hardware), and that they need practical experience with different types of pupils; (c) that there may be some points of psychological or other 'theory' — perhaps even Piaget — that they need to learn in order to teach X or Y efficiently. But that is far from the end of the matter.

The main point is that students can and do have doctrinaire views and feelings about the subject they teach (and, in consequence, about how to teach it); and this is basically no different in kind from the sorts of views and feelings they have in other areas of educational practice. Thus it is entirely clear that a student's attitude to the subject labelled 'English', for instance, comes into this category. Does he go for grammar or creative writing? For books that are 'relevant to the child's social experience' or for the classics? What is his attitude to spelling and punctuation? How does he value novels as against epic poetry? — and so on. The point is clearest with the more obviously controversial subjects — English and RE are examples — but it applies to any. There are deep problems about *how we construe the idea of* what is marked by 'teaching French', 'learning science', 'becoming a good mathematician', 'getting a taste for history' and so forth; and mistakes about this, often discussed under such headings as 'the aims of X' or 'the objectives of Y', are made through lack of common sense, sanity, insight and sound judgement, not through lack of theoretical knowledge or enough man-hours of brute 'experience'.

Even if all students were entirely rational about all this, there would still remain some matters of attitude of the highest importance. Thus we know, at least, that a good teacher understands the value of his subject, is keen on it and wants to dispense it to pupils. But this incorporates a very great deal of understanding and feeling that is certainly not always present just because the student has, say, gained a degree in that subject (in any case, what he has to teach in schools may be virtually a different subject, even if using the same title). Just what *is* in principle valuable, or alluring or worthwhile about biology, English, geography and so on? *What* exactly is the student supposed to be keen on under those headings, and what can he offer his pupils as objects that might not only stimulate or attract them but win their lasting attachment? These questions are not easy in themselves, and it would be absurd to suppose that students have the right answers and attitudes to all of them just because they are committed to teaching them; yet they are of immense importance and merit the sort of treatment we have already briefly discussed.

Another basic point of organisational method follows from this. The important distinction is not between 'method' and 'general' work, but rather between (i) what intending teachers need that is (almost certainly) free from the necessity to go in for this sort of treatment in depth, and (ii) what they need that requires such treatment. Items in (i) might include a good deal of ordinary, non-controversial factual knowledge that is not seriously liable to prejudice (facts about the school system, the state of the law, the teachers' unions, the way to operate hardware), and also a good deal of preliminary experience — getting around the schools just to see, preferably without blinkers, what actually goes on and what (superficially at least) pupils and other teachers are like. However, even this rapidly turns into (ii) certain areas of interest (authority, freedom and compulsion, the value of this or that subject, the pastoral care system, how to deal with parents, etc.) where muddled thinking and feeling, doctrinaire views, 'hang-ups', prejudices, fantasies and so on are, very obviously, the kind of enemy we have to deal with.

These kinds of things require a very different structure from the items in (i); just as teaching parents how to fold a nappy, or what child benefits they can get from the state, must necessarily take a different form from teaching them how to change their attitudes towards their children and the problems that arise in the home that are not purely factual or technical.

I turn finally to what might fairly be regarded as a much more interesting aspect of the problem; more interesting, because the points made above are for the most part entirely obvious (whether or not I have done them justice). Nor only that: a very large number of people in teacher-education and elsewhere can both see and acknowledge them as obvious — at least, if such people are brought to consider them calmly as individuals in informal conversation. Why then are they not acted upon? What is the nature of the opposition?

Yet again one must resist the monistic temptation to ascribe everything to a single cause. Various points are perhaps worth mentioning, of which the most important may be that the sort of teacher-education required — despite its obviousness — *sounds vague*, which to the BF is intolerable. Connected with this are various symptoms. From the viewpoint of so-called 'administrative efficiency' and tidiness it looks better on the time-table to put in a great deal of non-central material — lectures, film shows, visits to schools, discussions of Crucial Contemporary Issues, and many other things that create an impression of tightly packed activity; whereas the administration's job here is just to facilitate — to allow space and time for — the kind of work, perhaps more reminiscent of the context of Socratic dialogue than of anything else, that needs to be done. People in charge of institutions will tend to be 'administrative' or political thinkers rather than Socratic, and hence tend to underestimate (or even to have little understanding of) the relevant contexts. The apparent vagueness of the work (how do we examine or mark it? whom shall we pass and fail, and on just what criteria?) will alarm many, who will prefer to cling to such apparent academic respectability as they can get by bringing in sociological, psychological and sometimes even philosophical 'theory' and demanding the constant use of pseudo-scholarly references, footnotes and bibliographies; or else, if they reject this, to adopt the alert, trend-following, politically aware, pseudo-pragmatic attitude generated by the 'competence' model. ('When I say religion of course I mean the Christian religion and when I say the Christian religion of course I mean the Church of England' is paralleled by 'When I say education of course I mean the institutionalised educational system and when I say the institutionalised educational system of course I mean British schools in the present decade or, if we can guess the trend, the next decade'. This often tacit syllogism not only throws out such disciplines as philosophy, psychology, comparative education and others, but reduces even sociology to a kind of immediately useful market research.)

These attitudes, easy to despise, are of course understandable enough in those who have little or no experience of the more central alternative; and indeed there *are* aspects of education and teacher-education to which other approaches are relevant. We do not need Socrates or a psychoanalyst to tell us about the prevailing school system, or to give us immediately and directly helpful advice about classroom management or the use of hardware and resources, or to direct our students' classroom experiences on school visits. These are straightforwardly practical tasks, not totally unlike learning to write on the blackboard. Equally, we have to distinguish between learning to improve the mental clarity and sanity of a student in relation to the truth on the one hand, and giving him that combination of factual knowledge, shrewdness, patience, and alertness that will make him politically effective in the educational system on the other (though this distinction is hard to keep unblurred). But their place cannot be a central one, because being a good teacher is not centrally a matter of these attributes. Politics too requires a grasp of the good.

The central attributes and the kind of work required to improve them are not popular. Insofar as my experience is any guide, those who cotton on to them are not to be distinguished in terms of age, experience, academic ability or even intelligence. It seems to have something to do with the willingness to tolerate abstract doubt and to experience a certain profound dissatisfaction with existing institutionalisations (not only of teacher-education) together with enough security to avoid creating some dream world — such as a Marxist utopia — as a compensation. How precisely this is to be identified and fostered is an immensely difficult question; I am not sure whether we have made any advance on Plato either in describing the difficulties or in suggesting remedies for them.

If I have anything helpful to say by way of practical recommendations, it may be this: those who see the point should be prepared to accept and operate a dual system. In almost any world, and certainly in the world of teacher-education, much of our time and effort (and those of students) will inevitably be devoted to fulfilling the requirements of some system that will be at least partly non-rational. Doing this may be at worst harmless and at best a useful form of moral training. Within this system, when time and space allow (as they always do to some extent, despite the best efforts of bureaucrats), we may try to create and work in the sort of context, and with the sort of content, that really matters. The important thing is to make the distinction as clearly as possible, both in principle and in practice.

To take a practical example: I once taught a course, quaintly described as 'advanced', for a very mixed bag of students. The regulations and other official documents (themselves produced, no doubt, by staff members desirous of creating at least the impression of academic respectability) subjected the students to a mass of largely ridiculous or inflated requirements — the reading of three-volume books on educational sociology whose authors could not even write English, the amassing of references and bibliographies, close study of the vague and often tautological contents of government reports on education, attendance at lectures on the latest twists and turns of the 'Great Debate' or other political exercises, and so forth. The absurdity of this was doubled by the fact that many of these students could not even write clearly, detect nonsense for themselves, discuss in any tolerably sophisticated way or take up a common-sense position in the teeth of the various pressures of fantasy and fashion that beset almost every educational issue. I say 'even'; but of course the greatest difficulty lies just there, and it was just at that point where I had to try to educate them. However well or badly I succeeded, the kind of content and context required was very different from that supposedly in force. One had to say to them, and they to themselves, something not unlike: 'Look, there are the demands of the educational establishment: you must show some knowledge of the books on the reading list, write your essays in so many thousand words, with footnotes and bibliographies to make it look scholarly, and so on; now, take a deep breath and realise that there is *also* the serious business of trying to make a bit more sense, or gain a bit more solid truth or become a bit less prejudiced and doctrinaire, about these issues — and there are books (but probably different books) and other aids to doing this.'

Apart from suggestions of this kind, I have no immediate practical answers. How much progress is made depends, both immediately and ultimately, on how many people there are in the business who can understand and (more difficult) *hold steady* the points — essentially points of logic — already discussed. One is tempted to say that it would help if all or more teacher-educators had had experience of some relevant discipline: I suppose, analytic philosophy or depth-psychology. But many have been through such mills and emerged quite unscathed: there is nothing that cannot be institutionalised out of existence if both the system and the individual conspire to do so. Perhaps the most important thing is that those who understand should keep their heads, restrain their impatience, avoid the vices of paranoia or megalomania that tend to infect those who suppose that they know something important that others do not know, and carry on doing their best.

CHAPTER 7

Education and Identity*

I want here to consider a set of practices that exist, I believe, largely because of the RF: that is, those educational courses and curricula that seem to be built round the idea of students having a certain kind of psychological or social *identity* — an identity not related to their specific abilities or attainments in relation to some subject-matter of learning, but rather to quite different features of the world that seem educationally irrelevant, such as whether they are black or Anglo-Saxon or feminine.

It is easy to say that this exists just because of the RF; and certainly it is possible to see how a fantasy that involves not believing in the authority of a particular *subject*, combined with an egalitarian dislike of taking any particular social group or individual as 'superior' or 'inferior' (even in certain respects) to any other group or individual, might conjointly lead to this *prima facie* curious politicisation of educational practice. Instead of, or at least as well as, identifying students as students of mathematics, science, history, etc., we identify them in terms of their racial or cultural or social identity. But this requires argument. Certainly the idea is a very wide-spread one. The identity may be national, as in the case of emergent countries whose leaders wish to encourage national solidarity; credal or ideological, as with courses designed to reinforce religious believers or Marxists in their respective faiths; 'ethnic', as with Chicano studies in the USA; colour-orientated, as with 'Black Studies'; sexual, as with the studies propagated by the Women's Liberation movement — and so on. It is also a very old idea: in many heroic societies where the clan is strong,

*I am grateful to Mary Mishler for allowing me to use, in this chapter, a good deal of material on which we collaborated and some of which appeared under her name in the *Oxford Review of Education,* 1978.

as for instance in Anglo-Saxon England, much of early education involved teaching children to recite the names and deeds of their particular ancestors.

It may be thought, not without justice, that the notion or notions marked by 'identity' are so intolerably vague that no serious discussion could proceed without a lengthy and stringent analysis. That would, indeed, be extremely profitable, since one of the problems of most educational psychology is that it tends to be conducted in terms of vague notions of this sort, such as 'self-esteem' or 'self-image', which are certainly no more clear than everyday terms (for instance, 'self-respect' or 'dignity'), though these latter are admittedly also confusing. But I shall have here to rely partly at least on a semi-intuitive idea of the courses of study I am talking about. It may be helpful to say that these studies are characteristically defined in terms of criteria whose *original* application is not educational at all, but that have been taken over by various groups for psychological or political purposes. For example, we may, in a spirit of cool neutrality, distinguish various groups by the terms 'black', or 'Marxist', or 'female', or 'Aryan'; emotive weight is then given to these differentiations by blacks (Marxists, women, Aryans), which then produces 'Black (Marxist, etc.) Studies'. This is quite different from the cases, also common, in which educationalists create new fields of study for less personal or emotive reasons — 'Antarctic Studies' or 'The Technology of Tourism'. The reasons may be very various: some attempt to introduce variety, or some utilitarian pressure. These would, however, only be cases of studies designed to create or reinforce someone's *identity* if it were felt that tourists or Antarctic inhabitants (penguins?) needed their morale boosted.

Even if the avowed point of the studies is not to create or reinforce a group identity, they may still *use* an existing group identity. This is in fact so common a feature of many curricula that it is more or less taken for granted, and hence passes unobserved. For instance, it is assumed that British children should know more about British history than the history of other countries; the same is or was true of geography. Yet in other cases it would seem to us peculiar, or even a sign of insecurity, to do this: in teaching mathematics, for example, or science, or music, we do not normally think that children should concentrate on British (French, Russian, etc.) mathematics or science or music. We seem to accept these subjects or forms of thought as existing in their own right, and to regard any connections with group identity or national history as irrelevant. When they are forcibly made relevant (as when some British people refused to play German music during the war, or as when certain Communist countries stigmatise musicians or scientists as 'bourgeois'), it seems we have forgotten what counts as merit.

It is tempting to push this line of thought to its limits. Thus those philosophers of education who make much of the idea of 'forms of thought', or intrinsically 'worthwhile activities', are more or less obliged to say that it is the (transcendental or at least transcultural) *form* itself that should be studied; the particular instances will be relevant only as leading to a better grasp of the form. Thus 'history' will mean, for them, 'historical reasoning', and examples of historical periods or problems must be judged by whether they are suitable for this purpose — maybe a period of American history will offer more scope for historical reasoning, but if ancient Greek history is a better vehicle teachers might use that instead. What is important is the logic of the form; the fact that one field (period, instance) is closer to a person's immediate environment or self-image is educationally irrelevant — or perhaps only relevant as a point of departure.

Similarly, even if the 'forms of thought' idea does not appeal to us and we take our stand on some more substantive idea of what is worthwhile, we might still think that local patriotism is irrelevant. If we think that children should learn to appreciate actual works of art (as against the 'aesthetic form', whatever that might be), then we shall probably think that such things as German music or Greek sculpture or Italian painting should be put before them; not because they are German or Greek or Italian (and thus help children in those countries to be secure in their national identity), but simply because they happen to be very good.

In other words, we shall resist the idea that 'Because it's mine (part of my identity, country, class, creed, etc.)' gives me any sort of justification for learning or studying something. And this line of thought is demonstrably attractive, at least so long as we construe education as concerned with a domain that is, in a very straight-forward sense, *public.* Art, literature, science, music, mathematics and so on are not anyone's property; and it is precisely at the point when someone starts talking of 'my' ('his') etc. philosophy that he stops doing philosophy as a serious subject and reverts to ideological vested interests. It is tempting to say 'Keep these vested interests, the worries about "identity" or "faith to live by" or whatever, out of education; leave them for the priests or the psychotherapists or the contemporary sages; education is about public knowledge and public enquiry'.

Tempting, but ultimately unsatisfactory. For there are some things of which it is clearly true (a) that they are *not* public property in *this* sort of way, and (b) that it is or may be very important for a person to learn or study them. There are things that each of us is *landed* with. Those most commonly mentioned are such things as our society and immediate social environment; but a stronger case can be built on such things as our own *bodies* and our own *emotions*. Here it seems obviously absurd to say that 'Because they're mine' gives no kind of reason or justification for concentrating my attention on them. My soul is more important to me than other souls, not necessarily in the sense that I value it more or love it more, but in that I stand closer to it (so to speak). It constitutes what I am, not just what I know or appreciate.

However, if there is a point about 'public standards' or 'public criteria', it is a point not only about *what* I should study but about *how*. We have to insist that any student who is concerned with his own feelings, or emotions, or identity or whatever should not think and act without due regard for proper processes of verification, the collection of evidence and whatever brand of rationality may apply in this field. We have to insist on this all the more stringently, precisely in that such a student is dangerously close to what he is studying. If we do not, we leave the door open to the kind of irrationalism that expresses itself in 'reasons' like 'I feel it *here*', 'That's just *my thing*', or 'I just *know* somehow'. It is necessary to cling tightly to the ideas of standards, progress, mistakes, correctness and truth, otherwise we regress to the 'self-authenticating', and have moved away from the idea of *learning* or being *educated* altogether.

Much trouble has, I think, been caused by confusing (a) questions about the *justification* of studying this or that form or field of enquiry, with (b) questions about what is necessarily involved in the *process* or business of studying it. For example: there might be some very good, if severely practical, reasons why a man should wish to understand his wife and children, or the particular diseases that might or do afflict him in particular. Simply because he is landed with these things, it may be very important that he should come to understand them — important for his happiness, or his capacity to help other people, or whatever criteria we choose to adopt. Nor should we want to listen for very long to some philosopher who tried to persuade us that only things worth studying 'in themselves' or 'for their own sakes' were worth studying at all. In an ideal world, where we have all the happiness we want and feel no pressure to adopt means to practical ends, no doubt this line of argument has more force. But the world is not, or not always, like that: the practical pressures exist. However, if we now consider what is involved in studying these (to him) crucial particulars — his wife and children, or his vitamin deficiency, or whatever — it becomes plain that such a man is necessarily led to some *general* enquiry: an enquiry into the nature of women, children and (pretty soon) people on the one hand, and into medicine and science on the other. For, to put it briefly, these particulars can only be properly perceived and understood in the light of general principles. How can he come to understand *his* wife except by contrast, comparison and connection with other wives, and women in general? How can he grasp the relevant points about *his* vitamin deficiency without, sooner or later, grasping all the points about vitamins and the human body in general that alone give the phrase 'vitamin deficiency' sense?

In other words, insofar as he is going to be educated at all he must acquire some sort of identity as a *learner in general.* I mean, he must be prepared to relinquish the magnetic, non-rational attraction of certain particulars ('Because they're mine', or 'Because I just feel drawn towards them') in order to see them in a general light; and he must be able to employ the general virtues of learning — industry, accuracy, imagination and others — in order to gain any serious understanding at all. His initial motivation, as it might be called, for doing this is not here at issue; the point is that, however pragmatic or utilitarian his aims, he has to shelve his immediate desires and immerse himself in learning.

It may, of course, be true that — for example — because most cultures have been dominated by males, or whites, cultural products produced by females or blacks have not received a fair share of attention. But the criteria of merit for any such product will have nothing to do with its social origin, except causally. There is an ambiguity here that it is important to understand if all studies are not to be reduced to sociology. Jane Austen's novels are good because they meet certain aesthetic standards, and Einstein's theories are sound because they are scientifically true and important. No doubt some story might be told that showed how Austen and Einstein *came to meet* those standards because, or partly because, of their social position as being feminine or Jewish, but *whether* they meet them or not is determined solely by the standards appropriate to the subject.

The serious teacher or professor of English literature and science will not be concerned with the social origins of what is good — that is a question for sociologists; he will be concerned with what is good by the standards of his subject. If he is lunatic enough to discredit Jane Austen or Einstein because they are female or Jewish, we should say that he was not doing his job; and if male or Nazi professors have in fact done this, they need to learn better. But they will only learn better by coming to adhere to their own (impersonal and non-sociological) disciplines, not by being presented with pseudo-subjects or 'counter-cultures'. Any serious student wants to know about *good* literature, mathematics, science, music, etc.; not — unless he happens to be studying sociology — about black literature or pygmy mathematics or music produced by people with fair hair. A properly serious course in Black Studies or Women's Studies would lead, almost at once, to a consideration of various disciplines in terms of their own criteria of merit.

It seems pretty clear that, in practice, studies of this kind in education are generated for non-educational reasons: that is, reasons that have little or nothing to do with serious learning and the value of what is learned. The reasons are usually political, in a broad sense of that word: various groups begin to identify themselves, or are identified by well-meaning liberals and others, as 'black', 'Welsh', 'women', etc., and in order to prevent political trouble — essentially, to keep these groups happy and pay them off — the educational system is distorted by the creation of 'Black (Welsh, etc.) Studies'. I do not deny that politically this may sometimes be desirable, or even necessary: if the alternative to having Black Studies is social unrest in certain communities, perhaps the money is well spent. The question of how to balance political and other goods on the one hand against educational goods on the other is a very difficult one; nor is it made any easier by those who talk as if there were no such things as educational goods, thereby down-grading education to the status of a handmaid or ancillary to political or other ideologies. In any case, this question forms no part of my topic. Much more interesting is the possibility of advocating such practices on educational grounds.

What would such an advocate say? Perhaps something like this: 'Very well, education is indeed concerned with serious learning. But is not learning to have an identity — to find self-confidence and a sense of one's own worth as a black, or a woman, or a Welshman — perfectly serious? Can this not itself be an educational goal?' That sounds well, but conceals a grave difficulty that has to do with the concept marked by 'learn'. Briefly stated, the difficulty is that not every way of *coming* to something is a way of *learning* something. Whether or not students come to feel self-confident by engaging in such studies — and this itself is rather dubious, since it would have to be shown that the self-confidence arose (if it did arise) *because of the studies,* and not by being grouped together or given money or generally patted on the back — we should still have to show that they *learned* to feel self-confident if such studies are to be accepted as an aim of *education* (rather than, say of psychotherapy or indoctrination or advertising).

We can see the difficulty more clearly in extreme examples. Suppose young Germans, lacking in self-confidence, are taken over by the Hitler Youth movement and taught that, being of Aryan blood, they are superior to other people: what exactly are they supposed to have *learned*? Certainly they have not learned *that* they are superior to other people, for one cannot (logically) learn what is false. Have they learned to be self-confident? But their self-confidence, it seems, arises from and is intimately bound up with a false or distorted set of beliefs; so that, although they have no doubt *come* to be self-confident, there seems no reason to say that they have *learned* to be. We should only use 'learned' (and hence 'educated') if their self-confidence were based on truth, on a fair appraisal of themselves and the world. If a man comes to see that he is not inferior or valueless because he is white or black or yellow, we speak naturally of 'learning' because, and only because, we think his self-confidence to arise out of his improved understanding.

Much will depend, therefore, on what we think self-confidence or 'identity' *ought* to consist of; that is, on the appreciation of what truths or kinds of understanding it ought to be based. If we were to suppose, like the Nazis, that there were certain metaphysical doctrines that had both been established as certainly true and been shown to offer immediate reasons for self-confidence to some particular group, then we could count these practices as cases of serious learning and education. And the trouble is, perhaps, that we do at least toy with this idea. The self-confidence or 'identity' of many of us does, in fact, depend on occupying a certain social position, or maintaining a certain ideology, or having a certain amount of money, or in one way or another seeing ourselves (nearly always falsely) as specially placed in the world. So we tend to think that there is nothing wrong with this sort of basis for self-confidence, provided only that it does not (like the Nazis) cause too much damage or trouble to other people. Nor indeed is there necessarily anything 'wrong with it' from an overall point of view. If, to put it extremely, a man can only avoid intense depression and break-down by imagining himself to be Napoleon, no doubt he had better so imagine himself; but he can hardly be said to have improved *educationally*.

The business of simply offering, as in a shop-window, possible identities or pictures making for self-confidence to students and other people is not to be totally dismissed. People need 'a faith to live by', 'something to make life meaningful', or 'something to hang on to'. But this business only becomes part of education if these identities, besides merely satisfying the consumers and keeping them happy, also brings them closer to truth. A very large part of what, in practice, goes on under such headings as 'the education of the emotions', 'religious education', 'counselling', 'psychotherapy' and so forth neglects this crucially important distinction. It is one thing, and a very important one, to 'fix up' a patient or an ordinary person; but to do this by *teaching* him something restricts both our aims and methods.

All this seems to suggest that these studies can be justified only because they provide some kind of motivation or *incentive for* learning, not because they incorporate natural or otherwise important categories of *what* should be learned. Yet even this requires some qualification. Suppose that astrology is rubbish, but that people derive an important part of their identity from their natal signs, so that we have 'Libran Studies', 'Taurian Studies', and so on. Now one might say 'The fact that they see themselves as Librans or Tauri will motivate them to learn'; but to learn *what*? There is nothing for them *to* learn. So even whether or not the grouping of these studies is a motivation for learning will depend on how far we think the content of the studies to be true and important, how far we take it to represent something that can and ought seriously to be learned.

More weakly (from the educational point of view) but still importantly, we might say that at least these studies will motivate students, if not to learn, at least to put themselves in a posture to learn. Keen feminists will at least enroll for a course entitled 'Women's Studies', save money to spend on textbooks, pay attention to the lecturers, etc., just as certain extreme Marxists or other ideologists might refuse to attend ordinary universities but would be keen to attend courses in 'anti-universities' or 'free universities' on the sociology of guerilla warfare. Never mind (it might be said) just what these students are enthusiastic *about* exactly: they may be interested only in confirming their own identity; but at least they turn up and attend, instead of roaming the streets.

This is by no means an unimportant point; but its importance becomes clear only at the cost of seeing just how tenuous and contingent is its connection with education. For now we are frankly in the world of advertising, public relations or (in a broad sense) politics. We are asking the question 'How, in heaven's name, can we bribe/coax/persuade/stimulate/encourage, by more or less any means so long as they are effective, students to turn up and listen? What titles, or images, or packaging will draw the crowds?' Once we start thinking along these lines (and progressive educators have, in fact, been doing just this for some time — though in a sufficiently disguised way to persuade themselves and others that they are still behaving as serious educators), we have only two options: either to go all the way and hire a good advertising man, or else to reconsider the temptation in a much more general light.

The reasons for not taking up the first of these options have nothing to do with preserving the dignity and identity of the educators. If we accept that we live in a competitive world, in which parsons, teachers, policemen and other ex-authorities have to fight for the attention of young people, then they might as well fight with no holds barred. But do we have to accept this? The alternative, obviously enough, is to take up some kind of stand whereby educators and others are presented not as popular but as authoritative: whereby teachers and policemen are obeyed not because they are nice, 'stimulating' or fashionable but because they are empowered, and seen to be empowered, by the community to conduct certain enterprises by their own judgement, not constantly harassed by the views of students and the general public. There is a great deal to be said about how to make this sort of presentation effective; but to make it at all requires much more nerve, and much clearer heads, than are apparent in most liberal and guilt-ridden societies today.

But the kind of authoritative presentation we need is not likely to stand up under pressure (and in one way *ought* not to stand up) unless it covers enough, and the right sort of, educational ground. The need to acquire some kind of psychological security, an 'identity', sufficient self-esteem to keep going in a hard world, enough control over and satisfaction in one's own emotions, or however we choose to describe it, *is* of course a genuine need. Insofar as this can be done by learning, it is a genuinely educational need. An authority might say, as in effect authorities (and their dependent educationalists) have been saying for too long, 'Forget about your emotional problems and "identity". Buckle down to the learning of academic forms of thought, practise being a good Christian (Marxist, Buddhist, etc.), and that should suffice you'. But this could be attacked, either on the grounds that it attempts no serious education in this area at all, and/or on the grounds that it supposes adherence to current creeds or ideologies to be a sufficient way of dealing with the problem. But equally it is no good, and does much harm, to allow this *particular* aspect of education, important though it is, to infect *every* educational arrangement; to turn mathematics into 'black mathematics', or to allow the teaching of English literature to become a kind of amateur group therapy. These moves suggest the systematic guilt of those who, having seen the need for the education of the emotions but having failed to do something definitive and circumscribed about it, placate their own consciences by allowing it to enter and confuse (if not corrupt) quite different educational activities.

What we have to do, therefore, is to take this business seriously in its own right. If all our students were so enthusiastic about learning, about the study of subjects divorced from their own particular problems and emotional worries, that they could enjoy a wholly satisfactory identity simply as learners, we should have no problem; but that is not, and never will be, the case. Equally, if all our students were *so* mentally distraught and insecure that they could learn nothing of these public, impersonal subjects, no doubt we should focus nearly all our efforts on making them sufficiently at home with themselves to learn something later — as, indeed, we do with psychotic and maladjusted children. But the facts do not point so dramatically in either direction. We have to consider this kind of education as *one,* but only one, of our tasks.

Once we do this it becomes obviously absurd to start off with the assumption that certain students' identity *must*, or *ought to*, be framed in accordance with the kind of criteria that demarcate these studies. Why should they see themselves primarily as black, or feminine, or Marxist? It might be, indeed, that the cultural background of certain groups makes it likely that many individuals will, in point of fact, arrive at the course with some such framework of identity; but that would merely give the educators a starting-point, *away* from which they might want to direct the students.

I am arguing, then, that studies of this kind represent a feeble-minded and superficial attempt to solve a real problem. Those who might roughly be labelled 'traditionalists' or 'authoritarians' are mistaken if they suppose the problem is not real, or should not be dealt with educationally (leaving it, perhaps, to the priest or the psychiatrist). It is not only impractical but intellectually obtuse to suppose that we can, in a modern and pluralist society, simply carry on educating our students without paying direct attention to the problem of their emotional security and identity — hoping, perhaps, in some vague way that the 'spirit of the community', or 'pastoral care', or 'informal relationships' will take care of the matter. Something much more specific is needed. But equally it is feeble-minded to assume that the problem can be solved by playing along with fashionable criteria of identity conceived in social or political terms: in terms of being black, or Welsh, or a woman. To do that is simply to re-echo the students' own neuroses, to assume that by some kind of administrative or political or social rearrangements we shall solve our (much more deep-rooted) psychological problems.

CHAPTER 8

Motivation and Teaching

I want finally to consider an extremely difficult area, about which I hope only to say enough to prevent us from falling victim to the grosser expressions of fantasy. Roughly speaking, the BF (which I shall not be dealing with at length in this context) might lead us to regard the most efficient kind of motivation — perhaps ultimately all motivation — as at an essentially 'behavioural', one might say animal-type, level: to do with electric shocks, rats, conditioning and so forth. The RF, which flourishes much more in most liberal circles, reacts sharply against this by insisting that the only, or at least the best, motivation is or should be something much more high-minded or 'intrinsic'. Fighting our way through the problem is, I think, basically a matter of not selling out to either of these fantasies.

The term 'motivation' itself, or at least the way in which it has come to be used as a general title for the origins of human behaviour, seems to be a by-product of the BF. It is as if men were seen as vehicles, requiring injections of 'motivation' if they are to produce 'behaviour' rather as cars require injections of fuel if they are to move. Part of the same fantasy is the idea that people do things in the same way that machines do things: there is some push or pull (or 'drive') on the one hand, and on the other some overt, photographable piece of 'behaviour' that corresponds to it.

Many of the most important educational objectives — the most important things that people need to learn — are not connected with the strong, quasi-physical sense of 'doing' at all. Thus one may learn to enjoy good music, to share companionable silences, to love one's neighbour, to relax, to find pleasure in gardening, and so forth. In

109

such cases something like an *attitude*, or at least an *appreciation* of some *species boni*, forms the central part of the objective; what a man may *do* as a result of the attitude may be peripheral. Here 'motivation' is even more out of place: a question like 'What is his motivation for enjoying the late Beethoven quartets?' barely makes sense (nor is 'What is his motive. . .?' any better). If we rephrase it to read 'What is it *about* the quartets that gives him enjoyment?' we are clearly in a different line of business: we have somehow to connect certain qualities in the quartets with certain standard interests in human beings generally and in this particular person — and if this sort of enquiry is regarded as 'psychological', that term will now bear a very different sense from the one that normally applies in studies of motivation.

Indeed the argument can be pressed a good deal further: for just how much is this quasi-physical sense of 'doing' really connected with *educational* objectives at all? Of course it *is* connected, and importantly: children may be 'motivated' to control their tempers, sit down quietly, take books out of libraries, win prizes, recite their tables, and so on; most of these quasi-physical actions do no more than set the stage for kinds of 'doing' that, precisely by being more closely tied to learning, understanding and appreciation, are less closely tied to the idea of motivation. Coming to understand, or coming to appreciate, are *not* in any simple sense things that men *do*: they are, in some aspects at least, just as much things that *happen to* men — men who, admittedly, have put themselves in certain receptive postures, done a lot of work, paid attention, concentrated and so forth. (Nobody is saying that children should not be made to work hard.) In learning to do, or how to do, certain simple things of a quasi-physical kind, 'motivation' is entirely at home; but the further we remove ourselves from (say) learning to play scales on the piano, or to skip, or to recite things by rote, and the nearer we get to learning to play a Chopin nocturne properly, or to take pleasure in geometrical proofs, or to argue intelligently, the more 'motivation' seems inappropriate. (Even the idea of 'motivation' for learning to read seems mysterious; of course there are reasons — many different reasons, some very obscure — why a child should want to read, but reading with understanding is not a set of skills or techniques. So too with learning to talk).

All this, however, is just by way of preamble. In what follows we shall do best to confine ourselves to *one* important question about motivation, which might be phrased thus: 'Are there general or conceptual grounds for thinking that getting pupils to do things for one class of reasons is better than getting them to do things for another class?' Of course this is very unclear, as well as laborious. But the whole area is very unclear, and it seems necessary to spend quite a lot of time in wandering round it informally, in an endeavour to see at least just what questions we ought to be asking. We might start, anyway, with how a sensible teacher might think, if (as is quite common) he is in a position of being able to get pupils to learn subjects ('motivate', if we must use the word) for all sorts of reasons — fear of punishment, a sense of duty, love of the subject, etc.

A common picture prevails here, which needs detailed examination. It starts from the idea that the best state of affairs is one in which pupils learn things as a result of 'intrinsic motivation', and goes on to suggest that the teacher should in some way 'lead up' to this sort of motivation (perhaps via a ladder of 'stages of development'). The 'nearer' a type of motivation is to this 'intrinsic' sort, the better; and perhaps there is a kind of hierarchy of motives or reasons for action to be constructed on these lines. This picture is, of course, common in psychology and sociology; but it appears to be also accepted by many philosophers. Thus Hirst and Peters (1970), who discuss the topic under the (to my mind, curious) heading of 'Discipline and Punishment', make a great deal of whatever notions may be marked by 'external', 'artificial', and 'intrinsic': 'self-imposed discipline' (p. 126), as against 'prizes and the pain involved in censure and punishment', is considered superior because less 'artificial' or 'external', and a kind of grading system is set up that allows of degrees of 'artificiality' (p. 127).

Let us begin by granting that, for the educator, an ideal situation prevails when a pupil engages in some activity (mathematics, etc.) 'for its own sake': there are problems about this, but they do not need discussion here. Now we immediately need a distinction between (a) the pupil's reasons for engaging in the activity *generally* or *at all,* and (b) his reasons for doing this or that *within the context of* the activity. Thus in (a), a pupil might be driven to do mathematics because he admires the mathematics teacher, or wants to pass some examination, or out of envy for his elder brother, or because he loves sums. Here it will usually, if not always, be appropriate to speak of 'motives'. In (b), we are talking about why the pupil (for instance) puts down 25½ as the answer to a sum, or why he thinks that the angles in a triangle add up to 180 degrees. Here, though there are of course all sorts of possible answers, we should rarely find it appropriate to talk of motives at all: 'reasons' or 'explanations' would be proper, 'motives' usually out of place. We can (just) ask what a man's motive for playing chess is (greed, desire for fame, or whatever it is). To ask why he played P—K4 is to ask for a reason or intention — 'motive' would only make sense if we could tie the move closely up with some recognisable emotion ('Well, P—K4 is a very aggressive move, and I'm trying to get my own back, I'm angry with my opponent', etc.); usually the reason is not a motive, but derives from the context and rules of the game itself, which make certain moves sensible or at least intelligible under the circumstances.

I want to stress the inappropriateness of 'motive' (and hence 'motivation') in these and other cases, for reasons that will become apparent later. Another class of cases would include, for example, the case of somebody doing something out of habit. Imagine a soldier on the parade-ground doing drill: the sergeant orders 'Left turn!' and he turns left; 'Halt!' and he halts, and so on. You ask him (insanely) for his motive, or even (more sensibly) why he turns left and halts. He says 'Well, you see, this is a drill, the sergeant gives the orders' and so forth; he explains the system and rules to you. Why does he obey the rules? Well, he's a soldier. Why is he a soldier? 'Well, all my family have been soldiers, I don't quite know why, really.' If one had to give a reason here, one would want to start at least by saying things like 'He just does', 'Inertia', 'He's never thought to question it', etc. It would be quite wrong to make any premature identification of 'his motivation' (e.g., he wants to please the drill sergeant, he seeks promotion, he is afraid of being punished, or whatever: none of these need apply).

This applies not only to soldiers but to all of us, perhaps particularly to schoolchildren. How much it applies will depend largely on the extent to which certain contexts or systems or activities are presented to the children as 'given', as something that 'one just does'. Children may be positioned in a certain way, and just *find themselves* doing mathematics, sitting in rows, playing football or whatever. I do not of course deny that there are things to be said, by psychologists and others, about why children acquiesce or fail to acquiesce in such cases. My point is that, for the practising teacher, there exists among his weaponry of 'types of motivation' a 'reason for doing things' of this kind: call it 'inertia' if you like. Here even the phrase '*getting* children to do things' is misleading: given a well-trained platoon, no sergeant spends much time in thinking 'How am I to *get them to* turn left when I say "Left Turn!"?' They just do it. So it is at least arguable (a) that educational arrangements should be such that pupils 'just do' engage in a number of activities with which they can be firmly presented, and (b) that thereafter the only questions that arise will be questions about why they make right and wrong moves, or get right or wrong answers, *within* these activities; and now there is not much room for the notion of 'motive' or 'motivation' at all, only for the notion of good or bad, perhaps better or worse, reasons for the particular moves and answers.

'But surely even when a person is immersed in an activity — drill or mathematics or whatever — he can be more or less well "motivated": he can be slack or careless or enthusiastic, anxious to shine, afraid to look a fool, and so on.' Certainly; but perhaps the most important thing that the operations of these 'motivations' show is this: he is not properly immersed. How, after all, do we judge a good soldier, or chess-player, or mathematician? Simply by whether he sees and acts on reasons appropriate to the activity. Carelessness or slackness or bad temper, the desire to shine or come top or be praised — all these are only relevant insofar as they help or hinder the person to act on appropriate reasons. In an important sense, they are not relevant at all: that is, they are not relevant to the activity itself or to the person insofar as he is actually engaging in the activity. For instance, if a football player loses his temper and commits a foul, or wants to shine by scoring a goal for himself rather than passing the ball to another player as he ought, what we want to say is not so much 'He has the wrong sort of motivation for playing football' but more simply 'He seems to have temporarily lost interest in playing football properly'. We want him to *play the game.*

If we now say 'Just so; and that means he's got to be "intrinsically motivated", we have to be very clear about what we are going to mean by this. If we mean only that we want him to be thoroughly attentive to the rules and principles of the game, so that we can describe him as 'a good player', rely on him using the appropriate reasons, and so on — well, we can produce this situation by all sorts of motives, incentives and arrangements. One can easily imagine someone being a good player, in this sense, out of love for the game, or because it is his career, or because he likes to see himself as a good player, or because good players are admired in his society, or for practically any reason. Very often, in fact, we may not know (and may never know) why; even the person himself may never know. In any case, if this is all we want under the heading of 'intrinsic motivation', it looks as if we shall not much *care* why — any incentive will do, so long as it works.

If on the other hand we also mean that we want him, not only to be properly immersed and attentive to the rules, but also to love the game for its own sake, this is intelligible enough. The point seems to be that, if we ask the person why he gives this attention to the game, we want him to say truly 'I just enjoy it and find it absorbing' (rather than, e.g., 'I get paid for it', 'I must make my mark somehow', or whatever). Even here, it seems that 'motive' is not the most appropriate word: if someone enjoys food, or music, or chess, or crossword puzzles, it would be odd for me to ask him what his *motive* was. More naturally I would ask him — and then only if his activity seemed *prima facie* unusual or outside the range of standard human interests — simply *why* he did these things. Enjoyment is not a motive: 'motive' fits only when we expect some tie with a more specific feeling or *emotion* (revenge, greed, ambition, etc.).

In any case, none of this gives any sense to the notion of there being better or worse motives. We have to distinguish this notion (whatever sense it may have) from the much clearer notion of better or worse *reasons.* This latter idea fits most readily when a person is already engaged in an activity. Thus, suppose that someone makes a particular move in chess and we enquire into his reasons for making the move. Then there will be (a) some 'reasons' that are wholly irrelevant to the game, such as 'Because I just felt like it', 'It makes a pretty pattern', or 'I always like moving my knight'; (b) reasons that are relevant, but not properly worked out, or not backed by enough information: for instance, he makes the move to gain a pawn, but the move involves losing a more important piece; (c) reasons not only relevant but better than those in (b), for instance that the move is the only one that will save his king or mate his opponent. In exactly the same way we judge the merits or demerits of a pupil learning (say) history by seeing whether the reasons he gives for his opinions measure up to the standards and principles that constitute the discipline of history. If he relies ignorantly on a bad source — well, at least it is *a* source and gives him *some* sort of reason for his opinion; but not so good a reason as a more reliable source. If he ascribes historical events to the influence of the stars, we say perhaps that he is not doing history at all, or doing it so badly as to be barely recognisable as a historian rather than an astrologer — just as the chess-player who makes a move because he likes to arrange the pieces in a certain aesthetic pattern is engaged in art, not chess.

If good or bad reasons depend on the standards inherent in particular activities, let us now see what can be meant by describing reasons for entering an activity as a whole as 'better' or 'worse'. Let us go back to what Hirst and Peters say about 'discipline': that is, in English, about different kinds of reasons or motives a child may have for doing something. They use the example of a child who learns to write neatly because he admires a teacher who writes neatly (1970, p. 126); and this can perhaps stand as an example of an 'activity', namely 'good writing', that will have its own internal rules and standards. This case is said to be 'intermediary' between the 'artificial' incentives of 'prizes and punishments' on the one hand, and more 'intrinsically connected' reasons on the other (pp. 126-7). We will suppose, for the sake of simplicity, three reasons: (i) the child hates writing but does it because he gets beaten otherwise; (ii) he does it out of admiration for the teacher; (iii) he does it because he is curious about writing itself.

First of all, it seems clear that if we are talking about *good reasons for learning to write properly,* then *none* of these is a very plausible candidate. Such reasons surely have something to do either with the usefulness of clear writing and/or with the inherent aesthetic or other interest of it: one can easily imagine a teacher quoting these to a bored or lazy child. Of the three reasons quoted above, (i) involves the major premiss 'Avoid pain', (ii) the premiss 'Imitate what you admire', and (iii) the premiss 'Satisfy your curiosity'. But what we want is a premiss like 'Learn what is useful and/or inherently interesting'. That (we might say) is *the* (or 'the right', or 'the proper') reason or justification for learning to write.

To this it might be objected that the other reasons and syllogisms ((i), (ii) and (iii) above) are, after all, perfectly sound for what they are. Avoiding pain is justifiable, and if to avoid pain I have to learn to write, then I have a perfectly good justification for learning to write. We have a feeling of dissatisfaction about this, certainly connected with what Peters describes as an 'instrumental attitude' to learning (e.g. in Dearden *et al.,* 1972, pp. 3 ff.); but it is not at all easy to pin down. We feel inclined to say that *my* justification ought to coincide with *the* justification; or that *what* is being justified is viewed so differently that it is not really the same thing at all — it is viewed *sub specie boni alicuius,* but not the right *bonum.* For instance, suppose a doctor prescribes bicarbonate of soda for me (as a means of lessening stomach acidity). Then (a) I can operate the syllogism 'Do what the doctor says: the doctor says "Take bicarbonate"; therefore take bicarbonate', and I can do this without any understanding of the merits of bicarbonate as an alkali in overcoming my acidity, or even without understanding what 'bicarbonate' or 'alkali' *mean* — I just go to the chemist's and buy some; or (b) I can operate syllogisms like 'Do what promotes health: as the doctor has explained, you have excess acidity, which alkali in the form of bicarbonate reduces, etc.; therefore take bicarbonate', and now the conclusion 'take bicarbonate' will in an important sense be a different conclusion from the one in (a). In (a) 'bicarbonate' really means no more than 'what the doctor ordered'; in (b), it means more. Similarly one might argue that 'writing' is viewed differently by the pupil, depending on what syllogism he operates to justify learning it; so too a chess move may be played for all sorts of different reasons, and hence *seen* quite differently — even though the move is always describable as (say) P—K4, its appearance as a good or bad move will vary with the reasons.

If we keep our eyes firmly fixed on what I have called 'the' justification, it is very hard to see in what sense any motives can be relevant at all — other than the 'motive' to do the right thing for the right reasons (if, as Kant tried to do, we allow this as a motive). We want the child to learn to write, and also to see the inherent interest and/or usefulness of writing. Obviously this could in principle occur in many different ways: thus we might first persuade him of the reasons, and then (having seen the force of these for himself) he works away at it; or we just get him into the use and habit of writing, and later on he comes to see the force of the reasons; or perhaps both aspects interlock in a more complex way. But what has his fear of being beaten, or his admiration of a calligraphic teacher, or even his curiosity, got to do with this process? Of course we at once want to say that there may be *contingent* connections between these feelings and motives and our own educational aims: maybe curiosity, in point of hard empirical fact, leads pupils to grasp the inherent interest of things quicker than fear or admiration do; and maybe fear will get pupils into the use and habit of writing and other activities quicker than curiosity, and so on. But maybe not: we don't know, and clearly there will be enormous variations depending on individual pupils, teachers, subjects and so forth. And none of this establishes any conceptual or logical connections.

'The case of copying the handwriting of an admired person is an intermediary case because the connection between the handwriting and the object of admiration is very close. . . the connection is not nearly so artificial as in the other obvious cases of externally imposed discipline' (Hirst and Peters, 1970, p. 126). But what *sort* of connection is this? We have child A, who operates on the premiss 'Avoid pain', and child B, who operates on 'Imitate what you admire'. 'Writing', we might say, for A will mean or be seen as 'a thing you do to avoid pain', and for B 'a case of being like Mr. X'. There is surely *no conceptual* connection between either of these and the desired premiss 'Learn what is interesting and/or useful'. The connection to which Hirst and Peters seem to point is (so far as I can see) something to do with 'naturalness': that is, if I admire a man and want to write as he does, this is a 'natural' thing and requires no specially designed ('artificial') connections to be established, whereas if I only want to write because teachers will punish me if I don't, this requires special social arrangements (a person is given the social role of teacher with special powers of punishing, beating, etc.). Beating and writing are only socially connected, by a particular social context; admiring and writing are more naturally connected.

But this may be a wrong interpretation. Another possible criterion for 'artificiality' might be the degree to which the original reason is connected with *writing* rather than anything else. Thus suppose the reason was something like 'Avoid the pain of being misunderstood when trying to communicate by marks on paper' rather than just 'Avoid pain': the connection might be said to be less 'artificial', less like what Hirst and Peters have in mind when they talk of 'very general objects of desire or aversion that are tacked on in an artificial way to what has to be learnt', so that 'in learning what has to be learnt the child is learning an irrelevant connection' (1970, p. 126). Here we are back to the idea of relevant or proper reasons.

Rather than attempting to interpret this and similar passages (which I admit to finding very hard to understand) in a more minuscule way, we may perhaps be justified in trying a more direct approach. Suppose we say: 'All children start by being "on the outside" (as Peters puts it) of the various activities into which we want to "initiate" them. We have to get them (a) to see the proper reasons for pursuing them, (b) to pursue them, and (c), if possible, somehow to marry (a) and (b) up so that they do actually pursue them for those proper reasons. How we may most efficiently do this is an empirical question. *Prima facie*, however, (a) is just a matter of explaining properly to the pupils, (b) a matter of immersing them by hook or crook — and *any* kind of motivation may do for this, so long as it works and does no irreversible damage to them — in the activities, and (c) a matter of inculcating certain very general qualities (if we know how) in pupils, which we might summarise as "being prepared to act on good reasons".' Is there anything wrong with this?

I submit that nothing is wrong. What tempts us to think otherwise is perhaps a confusion between two quite different notions marked by 'intrinsic' ('artificial', etc.). Suppose a child sees some writing and thinks 'I wonder what those funny marks are', and then perhaps he tries to imitate them. We think, 'Aha, that's fine, he's "intrinsically motivated", much better than some "artificial" set-up in which he's forced to write', etc. But of course the child is nowhere near wanting to learn to write for *its* own sake: he does not even yet know what writing *is*; he is just curious about some marks. Using his curiosity is *one* way of getting him to find out what writing is; using his fear, desire for praise, etc. are others. So then we fall back on the sense of 'intrinsic' that relates not to the subject but to the person: we say 'All right, granted that child A (who is curious) is no nearer understanding and loving writing as such than child B (who is anxious to avoid pain), nevertheless child A's "motivation" is more "intrinsic" in that it is more part of himself, more "internal" or "inside him". And that must be a good thing.'

This sounds well, but perhaps we should first ask whether even this sense of 'intrinsic' really works; for (as Hirst and Peters clearly see) a child's fear is just as much 'part of' him as his curiosity. Now we feel tempted to say 'Yes, but his curiosity would still "motivate" him even if there were no "external" system of teachers punishing, etc., whereas child B will drop his desire to read as soon as he leaves school'. But maybe curiosity can fluctuate as well as fear. If we are talking now, not about what kinds of feelings are most 'internal' to a person but about what kinds are most *lasting* or most immune from the changes and chances of this mortal life — well, this seems a very open question. The important thing seems to be that we should make sure the child is thoroughly immersed by some (any) means. If there are solid and proven *facts* about some motives being more lasting, or more crippling, or whatever, then it will be time to listen. As yet there are none.

It is difficult not to think that a number of unspoken ideas lie behind the dislike of 'artificiality' — almost as if people had forgotten that the whole business of sending children to school and teaching them is 'artificial' in the first place. One of these unspoken ideas, I think, is that some motives are *in themselves* 'better', 'purer' or less nasty than others — either because they are not so brutal (rewards are commonly thought to be somehow 'better' than punishments) or because they involve less 'outside interference' with the child. A sort of Rousseauesque picture prevails, whereby it is at best a confession of failure and at worst positively wicked to induce learning by 'artificial' — that is, person-operated — techniques; particularly, perhaps, if those techniques affect the body or 'animal' desires (fear of detention or displeasure is bad, but corporal punishment is unspeakable).

It is instructive here to compare the question of 'motivation' in morality; if only because of a commonly accepted doctrine that here in particular there exists a hierarchy of motives, which are indeed supposed to operate in 'developmental stages' thought by many psychologists to be inevitable and fixed in their order. Some aspects of this have been criticised elsewhere (J. Wilson, 1973); but consider the very common notion that some motives or reasons for behaving kindly to other people are better than others. Desire for reward or fear of punishment, for instance, might be thought inferior to shame, and shame inferior to (if it can be distinguished from) 'conscience' or a 'sense of honour'. But it is not at all clear why we should think so; particularly when we know quite well that shame and honour can lead people into just as wicked acts as can rewards and punishments. If my honour (self-image, ego-ideal, conscience or whatever) is built round the notion of, say, 'being a good Nazi', am I really to be preferred to a man whose only motives are those of expediency?

Certainly none of these motives seems to have any logical connection with the 'proper reasons' for behaving kindly to other people (if we may assume that these have something to do with people as such deserving respect, having feelings, and so on). None of the syllogisms would approach the proper syllogism of 'People as such deserve respect, kindness, etc.; X is a person; therefore be respectful, kind, etc. to X'. The premisses would be more like 'Do what will pay you', 'Do what the neighbours approve', 'Do what makes you feel all right inside', 'Do what is honourable', etc. Nor could it be shown that there was any *logically* necessary 'development' for human beings through this hierarchy of premises, such that they *had* to pass from using one sort of syllogism to using another, and so on until at the end they emerge as using the proper one; whatever developmental psychologists may have shown, it cannot be this. All that seems to be logically required for operating the proper syllogism is some adequate concept of a person; and there seems no reason why pupils could not simply be taught such a concept, taught the syllogism, and in various ways habituated to deploy it. Here the improper syllogisms just seem to be irrelevant; if we use them to establish 'artificial' connections with the desired behaviour, this is presumably because we think (rightly or wrongly) that we cannot actually produce the behaviour in any other way.

To all this it may be objected that we are, in fact missing certain vitally important if somewhat obscure conceptual connections. In their chapter on 'Development', Hirst and Peters say of Kohlberg's stages of 'moral development' — in many respects a typical case — that 'The order of stages could not be otherwise than they [*sic*] are for logical reasons in that the later presupposes the earlier and is hierarchically related to it' (1970, p. 48). This contains the idea, well known to teachers as well as philosophers, that there are many cases where a pupil has to learn X before he can learn Y (for instance, the concepts of 'king' and 'check' in chess before 'check-mate'), because Y logically presupposes X. I do not think that, in the case of either moral development or other types of mental development, these connections and presuppositions have been clearly spelled out or properly argued for; but it is plausible to maintain, for instance, that things like 'honour' or 'conscience' are necessarily later developments, insofar as they necessarily involve 'internalising' the originally external incentives of punishment, blame, disapproval and so on — roughly, you have to be blamed by others before you can get to blame yourself.

Even this seems to me very doubtful: one would be inclined to think that some psychologists see what goes on in the child's head as essentially produced by 'society' in a more or less direct form; what some psychoanalysts say about guilt, however, is a very different story. But my point is a simpler one: namely, that such 'stages' are simply *irrelevant*, except insofar as a tendency to use inappropriate reasons needs to be identified by educators so that they can know what they are up against. Various 'pulls' (expediency, honour, peer-group pressure, and so on) are felt by various people, in various societies, in various contexts of thought and action. It may be possible to achieve a clear classification of all these variables (nobody has done so yet); and it may then be the case that there are both logical and empirical truths to be brought forward about them. But what of it? All this would be relevant only if we thought it impossible simply to *explain* the correct reasons for moral judgements to pupils, habituate them to using these judgements in action, and (chiefly, I take it, by the education of the emotions) try our best to bring as many of their feelings as possible into line with rational moral thought and action.

This last point may suggest another interpretation for notions like 'artificiality' and another sort of justification for trying to discriminate between motives. On this interpretation, we shall be primarily interested in an aspect of education that (an objector could argue) we have hardly mentioned; an aspect that is not concerned with getting pupils to *do* things, or do them well, or even to do them for the right reasons. We want the pupil to *love* their activities or enjoy them. Now, what makes this significantly different, it might be thought, is that it seems to be a matter of coming to *feel* something about the activities, not just (or perhaps not at all) a matter of coming to *see reasons for thinking* the activities to be important — or even a matter of seeing reasons for thinking them to be enjoyable. I may sincerely believe, for instance, that mathematics is important and enjoyable, and at least be able to quote the right sort of reasons for this belief; but this is a long way from my feeling it as enjoyable (or even, in a certain sense of the phrase, my 'seeing it as' enjoyable). And if this is so, perhaps we may establish some coherent idea of certain states of feeling ('motivation') being 'nearer' or 'farther' from this state, as idea that has nothing to do with notions like 'having the right reasons', 'using the right syllogism', and so on.

For instance, we can (as we have already hinted) give different descriptions to the way a pupil might see the business of learning to write: 'a nasty thing that I only do because I get hurt otherwise', 'a nice thing because it's doing what Mr X (whom I admire) does', 'a nice thing because I'll be able to write love-letters to my girl friend', 'a nice thing if I get top marks, a nasty one if I do badly at it', and so on. These are descriptions that incorporate certain desirability-character-istics or 'appearances of the good', *species boni*; and we might well think that the first description — 'a nasty thing that I only do because I get hurt otherwise' — was 'farther' from the description we want the pupil to use than the other descriptions are. It is certainly very tempting to say, as we move up some putative 'scale of descriptions', that the pupil is 'on the road' to feeling as he ought to feel about learning to write.

But this temptation has to be resisted. Consider the parallel with moral action, which we have just looked at. Now it might be said: 'Certainly, if all you are concerned with is getting pupils to do the right thing for the right reasons — treating people kindly because they are human beings worthy of respect, etc. — then all the bad reasons are (so to speak) equally bad. But this is not what we are talking about. We are talking about something more like getting to *love* people, actually *feeling* something about them: morality is, after all, not just a matter of proper behaviour for proper reasons, whatever some philosophers may have said. Now, isn't it the case that, if we get children to "behave properly" out of fear or desire for a reward, they are less likely to come to love people than if we get them to behave properly out of — say — admiration or hero-worship? Even fear of a person would be preferable to fear of electric shocks or being beaten, because it does at least introduce the idea of a *person*. The point is, the different motives we use to get children to do things carry an important side-effect with them: when we say to children "Do it or else Daddy will be cross", "Surely you want to do it, Mummy needs help so badly" and so on, we not only influence their behaviour; we also present them with, and perhaps inculcate, pictures of and attitudes towards people — and these affect the children's feelings in important ways.'

Of course it is true that, to get children to love certain activities, we have to present them with these activities. A child who was given no idea of what mathematics was, but who just received electric shocks or sweets according to whether he issued wrong or right answers to certain disconnected questions (if indeed this can be imagined at all), could never come to love mathematics. But it does not absolutely follow from this that the *initial* presentation must be of a certain kind. To suppose so would be rather like supposing that marriage-partners could only come to love each other if their marriage was initiated by mutual fascination or attraction (being 'in love', perhaps); whereas we know it to be possible for 'made' or 'arranged' marriages to be just as loving. Similarly it is simply not true that being made to learn poems at school necessarily militates against coming to love them; indeed there seems no reason to believe that leaving children free to learn what they like by way of poetry works any better. What seems to matter much more, perhaps, is the degree of immersion in poetry — be the activity 'motivated' or 'presented' by whatever methods you like.

For the truth is (it must be remembered) that we do not know what makes people love things or how they come to feel or see them as interesting, delightful, absorbing and so on. Clearly, however this happens, it is not *just* a matter of external presentation: constantly saying things like 'Come on, it's fun, it's so interesting, you'll love it', etc. does not necessarily help. One thinks of cases of forced experience ('arranged' marriages, the chaining of two people together so that they *have* to get on with each other), cases where a person may suddenly 'take to' a hobby or an interest, cases where a pupil may have sweated miserably over a subject for years and then takes a delight in it for no apparent reason. What seems to have happened is that we have forgotten the enormous part played by ways in which aspects of the activity may interact, often in a wholly mysterious fashion, with the pupil's unconscious mind; and, forgetting this, have seized on the external or social features of the situation — the 'motives' or 'presentations' used by teachers and others. Teachers must (to use a more general phrase) *put pupils in the way of* various activities and immerse pupils in them; but it is still not clear whether there is any criterion for selecting 'motivations' other than efficiency.

Even if we are solely concerned with the child's feelings about the activity, we cannot entirely get away from the sort of syllogism that we used to describe the child's actions. For we do not *just* want the feelings to change in favour of the activity (which might be done by some early process of conditioning, or perhaps just by good advertising); we want them to change *because of* certain features of the activity that the child comes to perceive. We want him to say something like 'Ah, now I begin to see that it's not just boring, it's got so-and-so and such-and-such features about it, so I'll go on with it, it's interesting'; and this is, in fact, to change his feelings by some kind of syllogism. The difficulty is, as we have just noted, that we do not know what such syllogisms are likely to be — what are the 'so-and-so' and 'such-and-such' about the activity that are likely to result in this change of feeling. Of course it is easy to mention *accidental* features of activities that may appeal to children; but this hardly helps, since we want to change their feelings because of the intrinsic features. Thus boys may like poems about battles, but we want them to like poetry because it is good poetry.

So, yet again, we are driven back to the common-sense idea that, so long as we use efficient methods or 'motivations' for getting children to engage or be immersed in the activity, it does not otherwise matter what these methods are; all that matters is that the children are given as much chance and incentive as possible to see and react to the 'intrinsic' features. From this point of view — that is, insofar as our concern is specifically with getting children to like the activities 'for their own sake' — all we really do with our other 'motivations' is, as it were, to hold the children's attention, to keep them 'in play' so as to give the 'intrinsic' features a chance to work. Let the boys enjoy the poems because they are about battles; so long as they read them for *some* reason, perhaps they will eventually get to read and enjoy them for the right reasons. But then we must also be prepared to *make* the boys read the poems out of fear, or habit, or any other reason, if (only if) that turns out to be a more efficient way.

The feeling that it could not in principle be a more efficient way may arise from a simple confusion between (a) the initial 'motivation', and (b) the state of mind in which the pupils will subsequently be. Some people have the idea that it necessarily follows that if the initial impetus, and also the 'ultimate sanction' (as we may call it), which together ensure that they are 'kept at' the activity, is fear, then the pupils will *be in a state of fear* while engaging in these activities. But this is obvious nonsense. It is, for instance, some kind of fear of punishment that may make me keep the common law (to avoid fines, prison, etc.) in the last resort, and I may also have been introduced to being law-abiding by people saying 'Well, if you *don't* in fact keep the law, the police will get you'; but this hardly means that I go around feeling fearful. On the contrary: once I have been given a firm push, sustained as necessary by firm reminders, the rest of my time is spent in finding out what the laws are and obeying them largely as a matter of habit — really *without any emotion at all.* Arguably (though this is of course an empirical question), the firmer the initial push, the less emotional disturbance I experience later on.

This takes us back to our original distinction between reasons (motives) for engaging in an activity generally, and reasons for doing this or that *within* the activity. Of course this distinction is simple-minded, in that we cannot mark out 'activities' in such a well-defined way: they merge into each other, and some are sub-sections of others (as, perhaps, 'writing' might be of 'English'). But it does at least remind us, when people talk about 'motivation', of the desperate need to ask just *what* behaviour is being talked about. 'Motivation' unfortunately flutters about between two things we have looked at: (i) the notion of more or less appropriate reasons for doing things, and (ii) the notion of a person or group of people being under the sway of some emotion in a much more general way ('He has the class properly cowed').

With regard to both (i) and (ii), one would have to very naive to suppose that some single 'motivation' could conceivably be *always* appropriate, if we are thinking of initiating pupils into school subjects — or even into games. A person learning to play rugger, for instance, (i) would obviously have to master all sorts of different reasons for doing different things in the game, and (ii) would never become proficient if some *one* 'motive' or emotion prompted him throughout — even the limited range of situations in rugger are too complex for that. To speak simply, such a person needs a touch of grim determination or obstinacy to hang on to a lead in the score when under pressure; a touch of alarm if the opposing three-quarters are eluding him or his team too easily; a touch (more than a touch) of aggression in the scrum; and so on. So too in learning (say) Latin: fear of making howlers, delight in getting the words in the right order, an aggressive and patient approach to difficult unseens — all these and more are appropriate.

Yet another idea needs to be brought out here, if we are to do anything like justice to possible objections: the idea that the more 'intrinsic' and less 'artificial' the pressures, the better — not now because the pressures are not so nasty, or more lasting, but because in such cases we want to say something like 'There's more of the person *in* what he's doing'. Thus if it is I myself who am aggressive in rugger or Latin, rather than having to be cudgelled by the coach or shouted at by the teacher, or if I am cross with myself for making howlers and afraid of making them because I shall 'let myself down' (or some such reason), rather than the teacher being cross with me and my being afraid of him, then more of me, or my self, is 'in' the business. It is this idea, I think, that really stands behind the other ideas about 'intrinsic' motivation being more lasting, or more true to the self, or 'higher'. Without it (we might feel), a pupil or an adult is no more than a sort of animal reactor to externally induced pleasures and pains, like one of Skinner's rats.

There is certainly something in this idea, though it is not easy to see just what. To go back once more to the case of morality: suppose I am told the reasons for being kind to other people, and accept them; and suppose also that, knowing my own weakness of will, I eagerly accept some arrangement whereby I am kept up to the mark — perhaps someone invents a sort of nagging machine that gives me electric shocks whenever I am tempted to be rude or hit people. What is wrong with this? Well, we might say, this might be useful for getting the right thing done, but it is no way to teach me to *love* people, to *feel* benevolent towards them (rather than just performing the right actions). But now suppose this is taken care of in some other contexts: perhaps a psychotherapist or somebody helps me to see and feel that people are lovable, that it is enjoyable in itself to treat them kindly, and so on. Is there still anything wrong?

Some would answer 'yes', on the grounds that there is still a whole part of me that is not being exercised or brought into play. The nagging machine takes away the need for such qualities as determination, alertness, trying hard, self-reliance, etc.: I have all the executive work, as one might call it, done for me. In the same way, to go back to the case of learning school subjects, the objection might be that the pupil is given no chance to use his 'executive virtues' in tackling his subject; and this chance depends on the teacher using (or at least appealing to) the 'higher' motives that may affect him. The pupil needs not only a proper understanding of the subject, but also a proper notion of (and practice in) himself doing the subject by his own efforts; also of succeeding, failing, feeling regret or remorse when he gets it wrong, pride when he does well, and so forth. Indeed we could go further: it is hard to see how, if *all* 'motivation' were of the electric-shock kind, a child could develop anything like a proper concept of the self, learn to trust or rely on himself and other people, or pursue principles and ideals and interests.

But then, nobody proposes that *all* 'motivation' should be of this kind; and one might just as well argue that, if all 'motivation' were of a 'higher' kind, pupils would never get a proper notion of and proper practice in the 'lower' type of situation and its peculiar virtues — perhaps they would become unrealistic, 'have their heads in the clouds', be insufficiently alert to the 'brute' facts of pleasure, pain, power and so on (a charge commonly laid at the door of modern education). Similarly with morality: if in *every* case I relied on a nagging machine, or simply had to press a button to get what I wanted, the notion of 'what I do for myself' becomes thin to vanishing point. But this does not entitle us to object to the use of devices (counting up to ten, timely reminders from friends, 'God Sees All' hung over the mantlepiece, the use of a tantalus — even 'pricks of conscience' are in a sense a device of this kind) in *some* cases.

There is, further, an unexamined assumption here that these points about the general emotional development of the child are necessarily of great relevance to the learning of *subjects* at school. Yet perhaps it is not much to do with learning school subjects at all, but rather to do with personal relationships (particularly with the parents). This does not mean that schools have no job to do here, but it might mean that it is a job not best done by feeling guilty about 'the wrong sorts' of classroom motivation. Naturally, if school *only* consists of classroom teaching, and *all* classrooms are manned by a Mr Floggs who delights in keeping everyone frightened while they do their work, this hardly helps to develop the pupils emotionally; but this is probably a point about general teacher-pupil relationships, and not a point about the appropriate motivation for children learning mathematics, Latin and so on. What one needs to say about Mr Floggs is not (only) that he is a tiresome sadist, but that he is not doing his job as a teacher of subjects. Given whatever background is proper for emotional development — loving and firm parents, concerned but sensible housemasters, or whatever — it might be very beneficial for pupils to learn mathematics from a rather severe teacher: his severity, if directed towards more efficient mathematics, would hardly be a disqualification.

And here, I guess, is where the trouble really lies. Just as it is easy to fail to distinguish between particular (good and bad) reasons for doing things on the one hand, and general emotional states or the motives that act as an initial impetus and an ultimate sanction on the other, so it is possible to regard the classroom as if it were supposed to be a cross-section or model case of 'the ideal situation' for the child in general. It has been argued elsewhere that, if (as of course we ought to be) we are concerned in this general way for the child's mental health, maturity, self-confidence and so forth, the classroom is not the kind of context we want at all (J. Wilson, 1972b, Part 4); something more like a house system, in a much more serious sense than most of such systems usually suggest, is urgently needed. If this is, for a particular teacher at a particular time, not a practical possibility — if there are *no* other contexts than the classroom available to him (unlikely, if he really tries hard) — then the urgent need is to distinguish those times and arrangements in the classroom that are devoted to learning subjects as sharply as possible from those times and arrangements that are concerned in this more general way with the child's emotions and outlooks. Otherwise we are trying to fight many different sorts of battles in the same arena, and are likely to lose all of them.

Insofar as I have anything like 'conclusions' to offer on this extremely complex topic (on which a good deal more *detailed* work needs to be done), they would be of a purely common-sense variety, roughly of the form: 'For the learning of school subjects, use whatever form of motivation works most efficiently; immerse the pupils and keep them at it by hook or by crook, whilst of course giving them opportunity and encouragement to pursue the subjects on their own *insofar as they can and want to.*' I stress the last clause, since it seems pretty clear that, in many schools, what pupils suffer from is not the wrong kind of motivation but the lack of any motivation at all. As yet, I do not think there are any *clear* and properly supported truths about some 'motivations' being better than others, though there are plenty of fantasies and prejudices about it. If and when clear truths of this kind emerge, it will be time for teachers to pay due attention; but not till then.

Postscript

I want to conclude here with some general remarks, following those made in the Preface, that may modify the impression left on certain readers by this somewhat unusual, and very imperfect, book.

First, I am well aware (having had not a little experience) that different sorts of people react very differently to the kind of enterprise I have been trying to conduct. Some take readily, perhaps too readily, to the idea that much of our educational thought is based on fantasy: these are likely to regard the philosophising as largely a waste of time. Others are impatient with, or actively hostile to, the attempt to connect opinions with fantasy, perhaps regarding it as a cheap or unfair method of trying to discredit the opinions without adequate argument: these might prefer to have had more, and more professional, philosophical discussion. Others again — and I have much sympathy with these — might see the enterprise as a valid one, but consider that it requires much more detailed, profound and professional treatment: they might look with tolerance on what I have written, but regard it as superficial.

Somewhat surprisingly, however — again, speaking from my own experience — much more violent reactions are produced by the readers' (or hearers') attitude to the *style* of what is said. It is not what is said, but how it is said — and, behind that, the sort of person they imagine saying it — that arouses the fiercest likes and dislikes, and overrides any question of agreement or disagreement with the propositions actually advanced. We all of us behave like this for quite a lot of the time; and perhaps it is only surprising if we forget how passionately, even in our 'intellectual' moments (as when reading books), we seem to desire friends or enemies, and how luke-warm is our desire for truth. Unfortunately this particular difficulty could not be overcome by a person-to-person, rather than an author-to-reader, relationship; for one reacts to a live person face to face with as much or more partisan feeling as one brings to a book.

129

Readers familiar with psychoanalysis will observe the connection between this point and the claim, made by many analysts, that a large part of their work consists necessarily of discussing and working through the 'transference': that is, roughly, how the patient feels about the analyst. I have not attempted in this book to conduct a parallel exercise, for two reasons: partly because different readers will have different reactions, but also because (unlike the trained analyst) I cannot even begin to claim that my style is appropriate, whatever that might mean — no doubt it is deficient in many ways, so that some readers' reactions are thoroughly justified. Nevertheless, it seems to me of great importance that, when reading or listening, we should all of us take some note of our reactions to style, and if possible try to understand why it is that we react in various ways: in particular, perhaps, what it is that we are frightened of if our reactions are hostile, and how we feel comforted if they are favourable. (It should go without saying that those of us in the extremely dangerous position of writing books or giving lectures should pay even more attention to whatever generates our preferred style.) For a very large part of what is said and written is not, in this sense, taken seriously. We do not listen, reflect and reply; we just react to some image. If the speaker appeals to us, we are reinforced; if he does not, we reject; in neither case do we *learn.*

Second, we might briefly consider what sort of work needs to be done in the future, of a less introductory or superficial kind than in this book. The only point I want to make here, though it is a very important one, is that we cannot get very far without much more cooperation between professional philosophers and professional psychotherapists. There is at present remarkably little: partly because each group construes its job as very different from the other, partly because such cooperation is not institutionalised (or very rarely) in universities and elsewhere, but chiefly (I suspect) because both parties have a somewhat narrow if not jaundiced view of each other. There is a great deal of misunderstanding about what philosophers and psychotherapists actually *do*, and why they think it important. Not a few psychotherapists share the view held by many laymen that philosophers are either just 'playing with words' or else just trying to dress up their own fantasies in intellectual clothing; and not a few philosophers take psychotherapy to be based on some kind of pseudo-science (this strikes me as an instance of the Behaviourist Fantasy), or disguised morality, or mere mumbo-jumbo. Of course there is much truth in all of this; but not as much as those who have these pictures would like.

Close and institutionalised cooperation is essential because both parties have come to speak different languages; a fact obvious to those who have looked at the (still rare) symposia to which both contribute, and an almost certain sign of defensiveness and sectarianism. One might almost wish that both would return to the less differentiated intellectual climate apparent in, say, Plato and Aristotle, and work on from there hand in hand. That is not to say, of course, that there are not in fact many very *different* questions requiring very different techniques; but it is perhaps to suggest that we have jumped too many guns in assuming that we have worked out these differences properly and have a clear grasp of what techniques are relevant to what questions. Much can be done by people with different interests in the human mind, provided they share a common language — preferably normal English — and do not retreat into jargon. A small and close-knit team of philosophers and psychotherapists would have a good chance of covering the ground I have tried to cover, and a good deal more beside, in a much more solid and profound way; any one individual who tries to do it must feel like a one-man band trying to play Wagner's *Ring*.

Finally, however, I hope the reader will not be too daunted. We have as yet no obvious experts or groups of experts in this enterprise: each man must try to be his own expert. I should like to think that I have at least shown that the power of fantasy is such that common sense — and certainly common opinion — is not something we can take for granted; and, therefore, that we need to understand and take to heart a certain kind of task. With the help of philosophy and emotional honesty, we have to fight a running battle against the corruption of our intelligences. We fight against heavy odds, and often we are defeated; but at least in fighting we act as human beings in some kind of freedom, not merely as the puppets of our unseen selves.

Select Bibliography

The topics in this book are so wide-ranging that anything like a full bibliography would be impossible. Accordingly, I have listed the books mentioned in the text, together with some others that the reader may find most helpful. For further reading, the best procedure is to take up the references in the books on this list.

DEARDEN, R.F., HIRST, P.H. and PETERS, R.S. (eds) (1972) *Education and the Development of Reason* London: Routledge

FLUGEL, J.C. (1955) *Man, Morals and Society* London: Penguin Books

HARE, R.M. (1971) *Essays on Philosophical Method* London: Macmillan

HIRST, P.H. and PETERS, R.S. (1970) *The Logic of Education* London: Routledge

MURDOCH, I. (1970) *The Sovereignty of Good* London: Routledge

PETERS, R.S. (1966) *Ethics and Education* London: Allen and Unwin
(ed.) (1973) *The Philosophy of Education* Oxford: OUP
(1974) *Psychology and Ethical Development* London: Allen and Unwin

PLATO (1970) *The Dialogues of Plato* ed. R.M. Hare and D.A. Russell, London: Sphere Books

WILSON, B. (ed.) (1975) *Education, Equality and Society* London: Allen and Unwin

WILSON, J. (1971) *Education in Religion and the Emotions* London: Heinemann
(1972a) *Philosophy and Educational Research* Slough: NFER

(1972b) *Practical Methods of Moral Education* London: Heinemann

(1973) *The Assessment of Morality* Slough: NFER

(1975) *Educational Theory and the Preparation of Teachers* Slough: NFER

(1977) *Philosophy and Practical Education* London: Routledge

(1979) *Preface to the Philosophy of Education* London: Routledge

WINCH, P. (1959) *The Idea of a Social Science* London: Routledge

WISDOM, J. (1965) *Paradox and Discovery* Oxford: Blackwell